Living between Science and Belief

Living between
Science and Belief

The Modern Dilemma

Charles Villa-Vicencio

FOREWORD BY
John W. de Gruchy

CASCADE *Books* · Eugene, Oregon

Cascade Books
An Imprint of Wipf and Stock Publishers
199 W. 8th Ave., Suite 3
Eugene, OR 97401

www.wipfandstock.com

PAPERBACK ISBN: 978-1-7252-6500-4
HARDCOVER ISBN: 978-1-7252-6501-1
EBOOK ISBN: 978-1-7252-6502-8

Cataloguing-in-Publication data:

Names: Villa-Vicencio, Charles, author. | de Gruchy, John W., foreword.

Title: Living between science and belief : the modern dilemma / Charles Villa-Vicencio ; foreword by John W. de Gruchy.

Description: Eugene, OR: Cascade Books, 2021. | Includes bibliographical references.

Identifiers: ISBN 978-1-7252-6500-4 (paperback). | ISBN 978-1-7252-6501-1 (hardcover). | ISBN 978-1-7252-6502-8 (ebook).

Subjects: LCSH: Religion and science. | God—Knowableness | Life—Religious aspects—Christianity. | Meaning (Philosophy)—Religious aspects—Christianity.

Classification: call number BL183 V500 2021 (print). | BL183 (ebook).

For Lwazi, Ollie, Naledi and Oscar

Contents

Foreword

I WAS DELIGHTED WHEN Charles Villa-Vicencio, a close friend and colleague of many years, asked me to write the Foreword to this timely and significant book. I do so, not only because of its important content, but because its substance has been born out of Charles's long and often painful personal struggle with the issues he eloquently examines.

Over the years, Charles and I have engaged in many conversations around these issues. We have not always agreed, and sometimes have disagreed strongly. But now in our older years when arguments, often for the sake of having one, are largely a thing of the past; when the challenges facing us in growing older are no longer to be anticipated but are upon us; and yet when we remain committed to the struggle for a more just world in a time of political stupidity, moral collapse, spiritual emptiness, and intellectual dishonesty, what unites us is far more important than what might have previously kept us apart.

Charles is fully aware that he is not alone in the attempt to relate religious faith to science, to defend or to debunk belief. Many others have engaged in this task, and he benefits from their insight filtered through his own well-honed critical skills. But his struggle remains his own, and it must be so for each of us whether we are believers trying to deal honestly with doubt, or secular skeptics puzzled by the enigmas of our humanity and the mystery of a universe which defies imagination. Charles has not confined his inquiry to the Christian tradition with which he is most familiar but also engaged in helpful comparative studies of the other Abrahamic faiths. In dialogue with leading Jewish and Islamic scholars, he thus provides fresh and thoughtful insight into the history of these traditions and their response to the issues.

And, as always, Charles finds himself, quite literally, in the thick of things where he has always been most comfortably uncomfortable. But that is also the place from which he chooses to explore the common ground that connects science and belief as a participant rather than an aloof outsider regurgitating the tired arguments that keep them apart. His aim is not to score points or take sides, but to find meaning that gives value and direction to life, his life and ours. For binding it all together is his own journey from faith to skepticism and disillusionment, his liberating engagement with secular humanism and science, and his slow but profound rediscovery of the mystery of life to which all religious traditions and scientific inquiry point.

John W. de Gruchy

Acknowledgments

MY FORMAL THEOLOGICAL EDUCATION began as a young evangelical Christian in the 1960s. It was during this time that I encountered a community of students, scholars, believers, agnostics, atheists, activists, reformers, revolutionaries, and cynics who launched me on a journey of exploration. At a deep existential and spiritual level, I have come to understand the African meaning of *ubuntu*, which teaches us that who we are is shaped by those around us—by other people.

The colleagues, mentors, interlocutors, companions, and critics who have influenced, corrected, and shaped me are too many to mention here. I am privileged to have learned from many great people, to have worked closely with some of the moral giants of our time, and to have engaged ordinary people—simple folk, salt-of-the-earth people—who have walked with me through times of challenge, despair, and confusion. I limit these acknowledgments to those who have, in the recent years, nudged me into a reflective, consolidating stage of existence, where I try to understand the many conscious and unconscious strands that constitute me. This includes a sense of returning to where my journey began, where I dared to assume I could understand and name the apophatic (unknown) dimension of a socially constructed "God."

The pages that follow are written as a *memoire* of an intellectual journey, within which the mystery of transcendence and immanence continues to prevail in the face of natural disasters, human evil, and critical thought. Related to this mystery is an inner spirituality that suggests a *concealed presence* that is bigger, more profound, and more intimate than I can fully comprehend. Experienced in solitude as well as the struggle for social justice in the rough-and-tumble of life, I respond to a *hunch* that there is more to the cosmos and life than we can empirically quantify. The haunting need is to ponder and explore the undetermined dimensions of life. Once this exploration begins, there is no way of turning back.

Given that I acquired a PhD in systematic theology and established a teaching career in Christian studies and ethics, my intellectual and existential restlessness was curtailed by a sense of entrapment in the proverbial iron cage, forged by a system of rationalization, resulting from religious and social control and preconditioning. I was drawn to contextual theology and encountered people, primarily in the family of the Abrahamic faiths, who participated in the struggle for equality in a deeply unequal South African society. We shared the same ethical goals and were often energized by different religious and secular incentives, each drinking from our own wells.

I encountered an ever-wider perspective on the purpose of human existence, discovering the same divisions between conservative and progressive believers in different faiths that I had become so familiar with in the church. I am indebted to Mark Braverman for his perspective on the biblical roots of Jewish liberation theology. Ebrahim Moosa and Abdulkader Tayob provided guidance and invaluable insights into the theological debate in Islam. I acknowledge their counsel and tuition with gratitude. Confronted with the growing impact of secularism and the sciences in current debate, I became increasingly interested in scientific theory and neuroscientific research, viewing myself as a miniscule instance in the greater cosmic scheme of things and the complexity of human nature. It is here that the seeds of this book were sown.

As any author knows, acknowledgments constitute a difficult task. I acknowledge the influence of a group of medical scientists with whom I meet on a regular basis over a meal. Their insights and skills in biology, anatomy, mathematics, and human existence have exposed me to literature and questions that this one-time theologian seeks to understand. They include J. P. van Niekerk, Roal Van Zyl-Smit, Dan Ncayiyana, Paul Clüver, and Anwar Mall. Peter Folb, Emeritus Professor of Pharmacology at the University of Cape Town, has been supportive in my writing endeavor and generously gave of his time to check the basis of several scientific assertions in this book. Fathali Moghaddam, director of the Interdisciplinary Program in Cognitive Science at Georgetown University, shared his experience in the sciences and social psychology. They are all specialists in their respective fields, so I take full responsibility for the portrayal of references and perspectives that they have shared.

My long friendships and working relationship with Alex Boraine, John de Gruchy and Barney Pityana oiled the wheels of my academic and social journey. Alex and I celebrated friendship with the regular breaking of bread and a glass of wine until shortly before his death. John and I continue to explore the outer fringes of our respective places in life. John encouraged me to identify my criticism of religious institutionalism in the greater struggle for existential meaning and ethical engagement in a rapidly changing world. I appreciate his support and the generous foreword he contributed to this publication.

Others who contributed to the thoughts that gave birth to this book include students, some of whom have become accomplished scholars and practitioners in fields of their choice. These include Tyrone Savage, a former student at the University of Cape Town and coworker, with whom a friendship has been forged through thick and thin. Nathaniel Roloff, as a former Georgetown student, has used his academic and community skills to enter the trenches of conflict management in urban gangsterism in Cape Town, Chicago, Rio de Janeiro, and elsewhere. Kat Meyer, a recent teaching assistant of remarkable talent, has contributed to my thinking and to this book in numerous ways. I further express my appreciation to other colleagues and students at Georgetown University where I have taught in the Conflict Resolution Program for the past eleven years. Foremost among them is Jack de Gioia, the current President of Georgetown University, with whom I share a friendship that began in the anti-apartheid struggle more than forty years ago. He has enriched my understanding of inclusivity and human justice across cultures, races, and religious difference.

No book appears without skilled technicians, wordsmiths, and assistants. I am specifically indebted to Margaret Rundle for her editing of early drafts of this publication; to Paddy Clark, who added considerable value to the manuscript and is responsible for the proofreading in accordance with the requirements of the publishers; and to Allan Wright, my internet guru, who sorted out many internet and technical problems. The final adjudicators, editors, and production agents of Cascade Books have, in turn, delivered a manuscript of professional and accessible reading.

My special thanks to my family: Eileen has debated my ideas, posed questions, identified indiscretions, and exercised valued spousal control. Our children and grandchildren have shown different levels of interest in my mutating thought. Each in their own ways continue to enrich my life.

Charles Villa-Vicencio

Cape Town

February 2020

Introduction

Known, Unknown, and Unknowability

Herman Melville came to see me at the Consulate. As he always does, he began to reason of Providence and futurity, and of everything that lies beyond human ken, and informed me that he had "pretty much made up his mind to be annihilated; but still he does not seem to rest in that anticipation . . . He can neither believe, nor be comfortable in his unbelief; and he is too honest and courageous not to try to do one or the other."

—NATHANIEL HAWTHORNE, NOTEBOOK ENTRY, NOVEMBER 20, 1856.[1]

MORE PEOPLE LIVE IN an interregnum between science and religious belief in the contemporary world than is often conceded. Some have moved beyond the reassurances of the faith within which they were raised. Others, having adopted an empirical or scientific outlook on life, continue to be aware of a sense of transcendence portrayed in nature; reflections on history; places of worship; the unknowns of science, art, solitude, fiction, and more.

The evolution of life indicates that the purpose of all living creatures is survival and procreation. The advanced anatomical changes and cognitive abilities that evolved in *Homo sapiens*, in turn, resulted in a creative sense of purpose and meaning in life as the defining characteristic of what it means to be human. "Why are we here and what are we doing?" we ask in the reflective

1. Quoted in Sagan, *Pale Blue Dot*, 49.

1

moments. Over time this contributed to human migrations, explorations, and empirical discoveries that resulted in toolmaking, agriculture, social customs, cultural developments, mystical projections, cultic and shamanic beliefs, and the birth of religious worldviews.

The enduring challenge facing theology is to find a space within which people, molded and formed through different traditions, cultures, and religions, can coexist in the pursuit of a just and peaceful world. Yet, evidence shows that the use of religion for political ends, in overt and subtle ways, frequently results in a deep-seated sense of religious prejudice in favor of the dominant socioeconomic and political classes in society. At the same time, the memory of a religious ethic, portrayed in the sacred texts and traditions of the world's dominant religions, is often used to mobilize alienated communities to disrupt the political status quo.

Within this context, it is useful to assess the role of religion in society in relation to Carl Jung's writing on the four stages or archetypes of life, namely, the age of the energized young athlete, the anger of the warrior, the phase of consolidation and social control, and the age of anima or inner reflection regarding the complexity of life: "Thoroughly unprepared," he tells us, "we take the step into the afternoon of life. Worse still, we take this step with the false presupposition that our truths and our ideals will serve us hitherto. But we cannot live the afternoon of life according to the program of life's morning, for what was great in the morning will be little at evening and what in the morning was true, at evening will have become a lie."[2]

Recognizing the continuity within life's journey, the perceived reality of religion is that the collective memory of the founding myths of each religion leaves its imprint on each new age. In order to regenerate the creative spirit of these imprints, they need to wait to be brought into conversation with modern worldviews. The recurring danger is that these imprints are appropriated and "owned" by both reactionary and anarchist forces in religion and politics, bolstering different tribal, nationalistic, gender, and ideological preferences. This loses the center of sacred words that transmit renewal and hope through metaphor, language, symbol, parable, and story—means that cannot be reduced to hierarchical dogma or popular belief any more than they can be reduced to scientism. It is the interface of ancient wisdom and modern discovery that offers an alternative to the threat of a predicted implosion.

2. Jung and Hull, *Four Archetypes*; Kelleher, "Afternoon of Life."

The chapters that follow address an emerging sense of convergence between the "spirituality of science and the science of spirituality" that influences restless believers and probing agnostics. This rapprochement is witnessed in both the intellectual dialogue between progressive theologians and scientists as well as in general discussion between thoughtful people.

Opinion surveys indicate that one in five adults in the United States do not have a formal religious identity, and this is partly the result of the growth of secularism and of scientific research into the origins of the cosmos or universe, into planet Earth, and into the evolution of human life. Parts of Europe and the United Kingdom are edging towards a postreligious identity. Developing countries in the West show increasing religious apathy, while postcolonial African and Southeast Asian countries reflect forms of nineteenth-century missionary religion and a renewed focus on indigenous religions. Islam is the fastest-growing religion in the world, and Southeast Asian religions continue to reflect traditional and cultural values in a rapidly changing world.[3] The membership of fundamentalist, evangelical, and proselytizing religions is, at the same time, growing at an unprecedented rate.

Short of taking refuge in a ghetto of isolation, believers can scarcely ignore the critical thinking of modernity that suggests religious alliances within and adjacent to institutional religions are likely to undergo notable mutations in the medium- to long-term future. To scrutinize, evaluate, and question belief is not to dismiss the contribution of religion to the gains of civilization; neither does the questioning of doctrinal belief imply the beginning of ethical indifference, existential nihilism, the slippery slope to atheism, or a sense of secular ennui. Indeed, the questioning of static religion is the hallmark of religious renewal, as witnessed in the Israelite prophets, Christian saints, and Muslim *awliyā* (protectors or friends of God). In questioning the dominant consciousness and populist beliefs of the time, prophets anticipate an alternative vision of faith that liberates traditional codes, symbols, and motifs from the control of those who benefit from and control prevailing social norms.

Doubt is the reward rather than the curse of both science and belief. It is the source of the almost unending wonders of science. It is the source of a spirituality that transcends populist restrictions and biased values that impose sexist, racist, and socioeconomic restrictions on individuals

3. Pew Research Center, "Why Do Levels of Religious Observance Vary"; Pew Research Center, *Religious Landscape Study*; Greeley, *Religion in Europe*.

and communities. Turning away from these restrictions is both difficult and often costly for traditional believers. Removing them makes possible a broader and more inclusive sense of justice and the benefits of peaceful coexistence with neighbors and strangers. Reflected in the great religious and secular mores of history, these values are part of our "better angels," sometimes only discerned in the wake of our initial impulses. Steven Pinker and others suggest that despite the apparent deviation from religious and other ethical principles, the twenty-first century has arguably been healthier, safer, and more just than any other time in human history.[4] This is seen in the advances of medical science, modern communication, and mechanized transport. Modernity has, however, also contributed to unprecedented disasters that include the opioid epidemic, cyberhacking, the intensification of air pollution, global warming, militarism, terrorism, and more.

This places a special onus on the humanities and the social sciences, the media, and educational structures, together with all concerned people, to adopt a personal and communal way of life that seeks to correct existing wrongs and anticipate future potential dangers. Central to the Abrahamic faiths is an ethic of the common good which includes the well-being of neighbors, strangers, and the "least among us," as well as our enemies. Selectively applied and often neglected by individuals and nations who are ostensibly committed to these faiths, the affirmation of these values may be the only credible argument for the survival of belief in a religionless world.

The biggest theological challenge facing believers is that of neuroscience, which explores the relationship between the physical brain and the human mind. Francis Crick, the joint recipient of the Nobel Prize for discovering the structure of DNA and a leading voice in biophysics and neuroscience, controversially stated: "You, your joys and your sorrows, your memories and your ambitions, your sense of personal identity and free will, are in fact no more than the behavior of a vast assembly of nerve cells and their associated molecules."[5] Questioning Crick's hypothesis that the mind is "*no more* . . . than nerve cells and associated molecules," others argue that he failed to recognize the impact on the mind of the social milieu, which includes socioeconomic conditions, culture, religion, and education (that benefits some but not all). Crick's basic thesis on the intrinsic link between the human brain and the mind is, however, a central feature of contemporary neuroscientific research.

4. Pinker, *Enlightenment Now*.
5. Crick, *Astonishing Hypothesis*.

The theological question is whether the psychosomatic quest for fulfilment, meaning, and wholeness is an inherent ingredient of what it means to be human. Saint Augustine's words take on new meaning within the context of neurotheological debate: "Thou hast made us for Thyself, O Lord, and our heart is restless until it finds its rest in Thee." It is here that the spaces between neurologists, psychologists, theologians, and secular humanitarians wait to be bridged. This anticipates a progressive, interdisciplinary brand of theology that is beginning to emerge and is discussed in Chapter 6.

While arguably having the potential to tame human aggression and affirm human worth, traditional religion goes horribly wrong when it professes a parochial or tribal god. This violates the historic essence of the Abrahamic faiths, each of which was born in rebellion against tribal gods and perceived forms of idolatry. In the complex age of cross-cultural exposure and scientific thought it is increasingly difficult to believe that God created humans to be the crown of creation, commissioning us to be fruitful, to multiply, and to subdue the earth (Gen 1:28). The danger of reducing God to an agent of tribe, nation, human privilege, greed, or gluttony is summed up in the words of Anne Lamott, who observed, "You can safely assume that you've created God in your own image when it turns out that God hates all the same people and things you do."[6]

Paleoanthropology, biology, and neuroscience define emerging human self-consciousness, and a capacity to reach beyond the prevailing physical barriers and cognitive limitations, as a turning point between Homo sapiens and earlier hominids. These, they argue, gave rise to a human capacity to ask questions, postulate answers, and visualize extracognitive or mystical images as reflected in cave drawings, abstract patterns, and symbols. The empirical implication is not the existence of God or multiple gods but rather an inherent dimension of human self-consciousness and imagination, which some scholars define as a form of protoreligion.

While Judaism, Christianity, and Islam all trace their origins back to a common set of ancestors, each has over the centuries been molded by geographical location, plus theological, technical, and social conditioning. Albert Einstein famously said, "Science without religion is lame; religion without science is blind."[7] Richard Dawkins, among the most uncompromising of empirical scientists, simply argues, "our scientific imaginations

---

6. Lamott, *Bird by Bird*, 22.

7. Einstein, "Science and Religion."

are *not yet* tooled to penetrate this unknown."[8] This reopens the possibility of transversal, crossdisciplinary inquiry that stretches us beyond our most self-assured explanations about life's toughest questions.

Fervent believers, unexposed to the undulating history of their own religion and the integrity of other religions, often dismiss scientific and related criticism of entrenched beliefs and religion. Afraid to interrogate their own beliefs, fundamentalists deny themselves the opportunity to be exposed to the insights of humanists, scientists, atheists, and agnostics, as well as to other theist and nontheist religions. Any single temporal take on life is, by definition, less than a comprehensive understanding of truth.

As the world becomes smaller and more accessible, an increasing number of people are probing the deeper meaning of the myths and allegories of different religions. They identify the crass biases of nationalism, racism, gender, and other prejudices within global religions, as well as the prejudices embedded in their own traditions. This is witnessed nowhere more clearly than in Dietrich Bonhoeffer's protest written from his prison cell shortly before he was executed by the Nazis in 1945. A devoted Lutheran pastor, he asked: "What does Christianity mean in a world 'moving toward a completely religionless time?'" He contended that there were people of faith who could in good conscience no longer call themselves Christians in a situation where the church had imbibed Nazi nationalism.[9] His challenge endures. Jews need to question the theological roots of Zionist aggression in the Israeli–Palestinian conflict; Christians need to probe the sources of Christian support for Islamophobia and global aggression; and Muslims need to address the religious roots of jihadist extremism. We've all sinned against our better selves.

The sheer horror and frequency of violent extremism executed in the name of most religions and exemplified in the name of Judaism, Christianity, and Islam requires sensitive believers to probe the sources of this violence. Sustained by metaphors of supremacy, patriarchy, kingship, and chosenness, monotheism has over the centuries often lapsed into aggression against those who hold different ideas and beliefs concerning life's ultimate questions. The initial openness, inclusivity, and transformation identifiable in the initial sources of religion have lapsed into the separation of institutional religions, as well as intrareligious rivalry, frequently driven by ethnic, racial, and gender differences. This gave rise to class

8. Dawkins, *Selfish Gene*, 200–201.

9. Bonhoeffer, *Letters and Papers from Prison*, 362.

distinctions between the religious elite, grassroots followers, colonized believers, and marginalized members. It further resulted in ascetic, mystical, and defiant believers who withdrew from mainline institutions in protest against autocracy and the privileges acquired through compromising with economic and political agencies.

The impact of artificial intelligence adds a further challenge to traditional forms of religion. History shows that religion changes slowly—often tediously. History also shows that some religions die while others morph into self-fulfilling extravagance characterized by individual prosperity, self-destructive narcissism, and nationalistic autocracy. Alternatively, can algorithms emerge which draw on the insights of science, poetic imagination, and enlightened religion to discern new levels of existential truth? The jury is still out on this question and the future trajectories of religion. It is nevertheless clear that conventional religion is undergoing a shift in perspective that Michael Dowd suggests is "as wrenching as the Copernican Revolution."[10] Fundamentalist churches are growing, Zionist readings of scripture are prominent in Judaism, and hard literalism is a formative part of Islam. There is, at the same time, a growing appreciation among progressive theologians in Abrahamic and other faiths who recognize that biological evolution, neuroscience, and ecology have much to teach theology about the source of life, human consciousness, and future existence.

Yuval Noah Harari argues that we are at the confluence of two imminent revolutions. Biologists are discovering the mysteries of the human brain and emotions, and computer scientists are developing unprecedented data-processing capacities which could shift human decision-making from humans to machines.[11] He contends: "Just as Big Data algorithms might extinguish liberty, they might simultaneously create the most unequal societies that ever existed."[12]

The good news is that there is an emerging desire among open-minded adherents of different religions to find common cause in seeking to understand the interface between religion and science. Social scientists, seeking to understand this intersect, draw on the long history of the religions in the West, the great Eastern-Asian religions, and the reawakening of animistic indigenous traditions to probe the reality of cross-cultural coexistence.

10. Quoted in Rohr, "Evidence-Based Emergence" (daily meditation, November 5, 2019).

11. Harari, *21 Lessons for the 21st Century*, 48.

12. Harari, *21 Lessons for the 21st Century*, 71.

The question is whether multiculturalism, empathetic listening, and logical thought can offer a viable alternative to an inevitable clash of civilizations.

Subjectivity is never far from any narrative. I wrote this book in an attempt to come to terms with my own religious identity, discovering how closely belief and disbelief are intertwined. Socialized in the Christian religion, I instinctively think within the principles of the Judeo-Christian tradition, while my exposure to the "masters of suspicion" in Western philosophy has resulted in my questioning the established practices of Christianity. In a more limited manner, I have explored the paradigms of Islamic philosophy and the insights of nontheistic religions. From this, I am left with a single takeaway: if there are events in the cycles of darkness and light in the experience of ordinary people, both believers and nonbelievers, it is (for me) captured in Jürgen Habermas's inexpressible "cry to the heavens."[13] In a world of critical thought, this "cry" has become a "question" the answer to which can perhaps only be accounted for in poetic and metaphorical language or silence. Provocatively John Barrow, a Cambridge University cosmologist, theoretical physicist, and mathematician, refers to the known, the unknown, and the possibly unknowable dimensions of existence.[14] Arguably, this is where to begin a transversal, cross-disciplinary debate on cosmology and human cognition.

In Chapter 1, the commonly perceived tensions, as well as the potential for mutual respect between science and religion, are discussed. Chapter 2 provides a brief comment on the salient methodological crossroads in the history of theology that continue to inspire progressive theological and comparative religious debate.

Chapters 3, 4, and 5 address the traditional beliefs of Judaism, Christianity, and Islam, together with the most germane historical mutations of these beliefs. These suggest that the hostility within contemporary religious debate is as old as religion itself. Fundamentalists cling to a literal reading of sacred texts while moderate and culturally exposed believers seek to understand the essence of founding beliefs in relation to modern worldviews. The elephant in the room is the challenge of modern science, which many believers struggle to hold in creative balance. Rather than task premodern science with answering contemporary debates on past modern science, this is returned to in Chapter 6.

13. Habermas, *Awareness of What Is Missing*, 5.
14. Barrow, "Unknowable Unknowns" (in conversation with Rebecca Goldstein).

Where Believers, Atheists, and Skeptics Meet

I know that many people are, or call themselves, "atheists" simply because they are repelled and offended by statements about God made in imaginary and metaphorical terms which they are not able to interpret and comprehend. They refuse these concepts of God not because they despise God, but perhaps because they demand a notion of Him more perfect than they generally find . . . We should not allow ourselves to be satisfied with any such knowledge of Him.

—THOMAS MERTON[1]

PALEONTOLOGISTS, ANTHROPOLOGISTS, PSYCHOLOGISTS, BIOLOGISTS, neuroscientists, and progressive theologians, the pope included, consider evolution, involving natural selection and random mutations, to be a scientifically proven fact.

Few can dispute that the story of the hunter and the lion is written from the perspective of the hunter. The growth of the hominid brain escalated from about 900 cubic centimeters in *Homo habilis* to 1,400 cubic centimeters in *Homo sapiens*.[2] Geneticists tell us that we share over 90 percent of our genes with the lesser apes. Ian McCullum, a naturalist and psychiatrist, writes: "All mammals (mice to elephants) share 90 percent of the human

1. Merton, *Seven Storey Mountain*, 191.
2. Wilson, *Genesis*, 22.

genome, with a bloodline dating back approximately 100 million years."[3] We share the primordial brain (limbic system), traceable back some millions of years, with the early amphibians and successive animals of the field. This primordial brain controls basic reactions, including fear, the fight-or-flight response, and sexual drives. The evolution of advanced anatomical changes and cognitive abilities of *Homo sapiens* only emerged approximately two hundred thousand years ago. This suggests a double human consciousness, sometimes referred to in relation to the left and right hemispheres of the brain, with the left being the primary source of reason and logic in the promotion of science, mathematics, and technology and the right prioritizing emotional and intuitive dimensions of consciousness. Paleontologists, social anthropologists, and neuroscientists trace the origins of human curiosity, imagination, and invention to the interaction between the responses of the human cerebrum to the challenges of life. Participants in this debate suggest that the enduring sense of extra-empirical awareness or transcendence, including multiple religious projections—ranging from witchcraft and astrology to anthropomorphic notions of divinity and diverse ritualistic and cultural practices—are often beyond rational understanding.

Atheists dismiss religion as superstitious nonsense while many among them marvel at the emergence of human dexterity and intellect in the evolution of life from the first elementary cell to emerge on the planet Earth. Probing agnostics are fascinated by the endurance of religious beliefs and at the same time are unable to make sense of the tenets of institutional religious belief. Perhaps the majority of people in the world cling to a transcendent something or someone, at least at a subliminal level.

At the risk of caricature, I note that this double consciousness finds a measure of affinity in Hughes Mearns's "The Little Man Who Wasn't There":

> Yesterday upon the stair
> I met a man who wasn't there
> He wasn't there again today
> I wish, I wish he'd go away."[4]

An eerie presence lingers in human imagination. Early forms of the Abrahamic faiths have throughout history been reduced to dogma, against which mystics rebelled. This is discussed in subsequent chapters on Judaism, Christianity, and Islam.

---

3. McCullum, "Pulse of Protest."
4. Mearns, "The Man Who Wasn't There" (1899).

Evolutionary scientists and historians of early religion (who include atheists, theists, nontheists, and freethinkers) concur that human compulsion to overcome finite problems, together with the tendency to explore hunches and project numinous images in art and ritual, are an inherent part of human evolution. The nineteenth-century founder of cultural anthropology, Edward Burnett Tylor, laid the foundation for the scientific analysis of early cave drawings, crosshatch lines, and symbols back to the Middle Paleolithic Period which gave rise to a growing interest in the link between these remnants and research on early rituals, often referred to as "out of brain information."[5]

Religion was once regarded as the basis of all information concerning the origins of planet Earth and the *extraterrestrial* galaxies. Today an increasing number of people look to the exponential growth of the natural sciences, with neuroscience identifying an inherent link between the physical brain and the mind. This connection is understood to involve a complex relationship between the billions of neurons and synapses of the physical brain and the social and intellectual environment to which a person is exposed. This, it is argued, contributes to personality formation, human preferences, and outlooks on life, including the existential questions concerning spiritual awareness, hitherto regarded as evidence of a supernatural reality beyond human identity.

Honest conversation between the biological sciences and neurosciences on the one hand and social sciences, the humanities, and critical theology on the other, needs to take the discussion further. An important dimension of this dialogue involves the exploration of the social context within which the mysteries of existence are entrenched. Social science identifies a herd instinct that brings people together through common values, rituals, and social needs, which change through successive generations. Significantly, the history of the resistance to these changes indicates the extent to which the failure to adjust to changing human consciousness undermines institutional renewal and survival. This is reflected in the divisions in many religious and other institutions concerning racism, gender, and sexual discrimination. In retrospect, some of the boldest critics of social and unethical complacency in religious institutions have in successive generations come to be seen as neglected virtuosi, while others are forgotten as apostates and enemies of God.

5. Tylor, *Primitive Culture*; see also Aslan, *God: A Human History*, 21–22; "Oldest Known Drawing Discovered in African Cave," *Washington Post*, September 15, 2018.

Religious Discontent

Religious discontent and social divisions are as old as religion itself. The Hebrew Bible includes the pessimism of the essentially unknown Job: "A mortal born of woman is of few days and full of trouble." (Job 14:1). He turns his wrath against God, before the redacted text includes his repentance, and a twofold reward from God of sheep, camels, oxen, and goats plus longevity. The Teacher, in turn, tells of having searched "all that is done under heaven," concluding, "it is an unhappy business that God has given human beings to be busy with." He also mentions, "All the deeds that are done under the sun . . . all is vanity and a chasing of the wind." (Eccl 1:12–13). The psalmists and prophets rejoice in the glory of God and the beauty of the earth, while warning of the wrath that awaits the wayward and disobedient. This is a message perpetuated in the New Testament and the Qur'an, while responses to these teachings are explained and often softened in subsequent theological understandings of these texts. This development, together with the skepticism of the secular age, resulted in the prevarication among moderate believers concerning the meaning of future punishment and redemption. The Fourth Industrial Revolution, building on the age of computer automatized information, is, in turn, characterized by a fusion of algorithms, designs, and technologies that blur the lines between the physical, digital, biological, artificial, and psychological spheres of existence, which are likely to further depreciate dogmatic interpretations of sacred texts. This effectively leaves traditional believers with three options in the intensifying critique of religion. The first involves the rejection of modern scientific insights concerning creation and the place of humanity within it. The second involves the dismissal of these traditional accounts as outdated superstition. The third involves the exploration of the nature of a sense of "transcendent otherness" in the experience of believers. This is expressed in storytelling, myths, and ancient memory as well as through humanist and secular explanations of persistent mystical beliefs in an unknown, ineffable something that science fails to account for in their lives.

The distinguished (sometimes controversial) Harvard-based biologist and entomologist, E. O. Wilson, views traditional religious worldviews as a constraint on human progress. "I am not an atheist [but] I am a scientist," he states. He suggests that "humans everywhere have a strong tendency to wonder about whether they're being looked over by a god or not. Practically every person ponders whether they're going to have another life." His concern is: "This transcendent searching has been hijacked by the tribal religions. So I would say that for the sake of human progress, the best thing we could possibly do would be to diminish, to the point of eliminating, religious faiths. But certainly not eliminating the natural yearnings of our species or the asking of these great questions."[6] Wilson's quest is for what he calls "consilience" or a "unified web of knowledge" that incorporates the scientific disciplines as well as the social sciences and humanities, and by implication the study of religion and theology.[7]

Wilson speaks of the human "love of novelty" and the "aesthetic surprise of unanticipated facts and theories" and the "will to know" that draw us into the depths of prehistory where life first began. He argues that scientific research is at the level of "proximate causation," while traditional religious believers ascribe "ultimate causation" to "the God of Genesis" or the "*mysterium tremendum et fascinans*" (a mystery before which we both tremble and are fascinated) as described by the twentieth-century German philosopher, Rudolf Otto.[8] Wilson's concern is that believers lapse into "extreme anthropocentrism" in seeking to understand any sense of "numinosity" or "transcendence" in life, which he sees as a domain best explored in dialogue between the sciences and humanities. This dialogue, he suggests, is the most viable option to explain the human will to know and understand.[9]

Jean-Paul Sartre and other existentialists argue (as discussed further in the following chapter) that metaphysical and theological probing of existence is best described as an exercise in absurdity or nothingness. His supportive critics see this as an "inner space" that amounts to a secular "experience of God's non-existence" rather than a philosophical objection to the several existing brands of atheism.[10] Kate Kirkpatrick refers to it as an endeavor to make sense of the "absurdity of otherness" or what John Gillespie regards as a metaphysical quest or "spiritual odyssey."[11] Other philosophers and biologists reduce this human quest or odyssey to the evolutionary process of human existence.

Richard Dawkins presents a compelling image. "Imagine," he says, "you are standing beside your mother, holding her hand. She is holding her

---

6. Osborne, "E. O. Wilson."

7. Wilson, *Consilience*.

8. Otto, *Idea of the Holy*.

9. Wilson, *Origins of Creativity*, 4–7, 56–57.

10. Kirkpatrick, *Sartre and Theology*, 4, 46: See also Gray, *Seven Types of Atheism*.

11. Gillespie, "Sartre and God: A Spiritual Odyssey?" (parts 1 and 2).

mother's hand, who is holding her mother's hand. On and on goes the lineage, each of you holding the hand of your mother, until your line is three hundred miles long and goes back in time five million years, deep into the African rain forest, where the clasping hand is that of a chimpanzee."[12] He argues that our ancestors, living in what was left of the diminishing rain forests and the savannahs, had no alternative but to adapt to their new environment. Although we share 98 percent of our genes with chimpanzees, biologists and neurologists ascribe the evolution of humans to more than genetic continuity. They explain human ingenuity and superior rationality, accompanied by a massive increase in the size of the human brain and related developments, to the stimulation of environmental change, the need to survive, improved nutrition, skills development, growing communication, and language development. The coevolving of the structure of the brain, retention of the emotions of ancient primates, and the skills derived from the will to survive resulted in the emergence of *Homo sapiens*, the distinct and most advanced pinnacle of evolution, as discussed below.

While reluctant to resort to traditional theological language, both renowned astrophysicist Carl Sagan and leading theoretical physicist Sean Carroll, with a measure of reverence, acknowledge the "vast unknown." They approach their work with uncompromising rationality, arguing that in the absence of empirical findings—critical observation and the verification of data—there is no indication of the existence of God or any related sense of divinity. They do not, however, exclude the possibility of future findings not yet discerned through empirical evidence. This level of empirical, scientific searching for truth ought to be welcomed by believers. It is an important contribution to unraveling the historic events in sacred texts and traditions that fail to meet the insights of contemporary research, which hard-line fundamentalists believe are too fragile to expose to unflinching inquiry.

Cosmology and the Origins of Human Life

In an interview Stephen Hawking, the author of *A Brief History of Time*, famously states: "We are just an advanced breed of monkeys on a minor planet of a very average star. *But we can understand the Universe.* This makes us something very special."[13] In a later interview he stated: "In the past,

12. Dawkins, "Meet My Cousin, the Chimpanzee"; see also Thomas, *Old Way*, 7.
13. Hawking, interview with *Der Spiegel*, October 17, 1988.

14

before we understood science, it was logical to believe that God created the Universe. But now science offers a more convincing explanation. What I meant when I said that we would know 'the mind of God' was that we would understand everything that God would be able to understand if [God] even existed. But there is no God. I'm an atheist. Religion believes in miracles, but these are not compatible with science."[14]

Progressive theologians face the insights of scientists and freethinkers with increasing interest. Charles Darwin's *The Origin of Species* revolutionized debate on the evolution of life, and it continues to leave its imprint on intellectual thought. Revised and revisited by biologists, it also continues to leave its imprint on biology. It is here that rigid disciplinary distinctions need to give way to the interdisciplinary dialogue that Wentzel van Huyssteen refers to as "transversal reasoning," with neither scientists nor theologians surrendering the raison d'être of their disciplines.[15] The nexus of this encounter includes several related discussions. These include the origins of the universe and the evolution of *Homo sapiens* as well as the biological cognitive revolution that gave rise to unprecedented levels of animal creativity, imagination, and belief in supernatural forces to which the origins of prototype religion can be traced.

Origins of the Universe

Albert Einstein's ideas on the capacity of gravity to bend light and his insights into quantum mechanics contributed to the work of Max Planck, who suggested an element of unpredictability or randomness in space. Einstein famously responded: "God does not play dice!" Importantly their work contributed to that of Richard Feynman, Julian Schwinger, and Sinitiro Tomonaga, who in 1965 received the Nobel Prize in physics for their fundamental work in quantum electrodynamics (QED). Reflecting on everything involved in the inter-relationship between energy, light and matter, the splitting of the atom and the curvature of space-time, Stephen Hawking commented that the growth and intensity of mathematics, physics, and chemistry is such that it is increasingly difficult for "non-specialists" to keep up with the advances in the sciences.[16] On the anecdotal side, Galileo is famously quoted as saying, "[The universe] cannot be read until we have

14. Jáuregui, "Stephen Hawking" (2014 interview with *El Mundo*).

15. Van Huyssteen, *Alone in the World?*, 41.

16. Hawking, *Brief History of Time*, 190.

learnt the language and become familiar with the characters in which it is written. It is written in mathematical language, and the letters are triangles, circles and other geometrical figures, without which means it is humanly impossible to comprehend a single word."[17] Einstein remained troubled by the relationship between the human experience of time and of time in the scientific worldview, saying, "only two things are infinite, the universe and human stupidity, and I'm not too sure about the universe."[18] Drawing on the probability theory of Thomas Bayes and Pierre-Simon Laplace, Einstein, Max Planck, and Niels Bohr would shape twentieth-century scientific relativism and quantum physics, providing a foundation for debate on how human consciousness relates to scientific reality.[19]

If theology was once seen as the "queen of the sciences," ascribing the unknown to the "God of the gaps," this dubious title has been appropriated in the modern world by the sciences such as physics, cosmology, geology, neuroscience, evolutionary biology, behavioral sciences, palaeoanthropology, and archaeology. Exponents of these disciplines readily acknowledge that they do not fully understand every aspect of creation. Carl Sagan, a doyen of the cosmology debate, stressed that, by definition, science is a self-correcting process, subject to improved methods and instruments for measurement and observation.[20] Some indeed argue that science never *proves* anything. The renowned evolutionary biologist and convinced atheist Dawkins refers to religion as a debilitating virus, while acknowledging that "our scientific imaginations are not yet tooled to penetrate" the ultimate origin of the complexities of the universe.[21] Scientists have nevertheless developed incredible insights into the nature of the universe, which include a consensus concerning the origins of our galaxy, planet Earth, and life itself.

Consensus among cosmologists is that the universe began with a galactic explosion (big bang) some 13.5 billion years ago. Five billion years ago the resultant subatomic particles and atoms are understood to have merged to form asteroids, meteors, stars, planets, and the sun, with the gravity of the sun drawing the planets, the stars, and other celestial objects into orbit

17. Galileo, *Opere Il Saggiatore*, 171. Quoted on the Mathematical Association of America website (https://www.maa.org/press/periodicals/convergence/quotations/galilei-galileo-1564-1642-1/).

18. But see *Quote Investigator* (website), "Two Things are Infinite."

19. See Davies, "Blind spot."

20. Sagan *Demon-Haunted World*, 407.

21. Dawkins, *God Delusion*, 407.

around it. It is accepted that our galaxy, consisting of the sun and in excess of a billion stars, is but one of at least 100 billion galaxies. Some astronomers project 200 billion or more galaxies in the universe.

Buffeted by interstellar bodies and subjected to heat and pressure, the molten planet Earth gradually cooled and stabilized into an initial land mass and oceans approximately 3.8 billion years ago, with microscopic single-celled living entities beginning to evolve. The earth continued to face volcanic and related eruptions and the breakup of land masses that eventually resulted in the formation of separate continents and ocean basins as we know them.

If the story of the earth is plotted on a twenty-four-hour clock, the earth emerged around midnight or at the beginning of a new day. Extending the metaphor, dinosaurs became extinct in the first of five mass extinctions of earth's inhabitants as a result of a giant meteor hitting the earth about 6.5 million years ago, or eleven minutes before midnight near the end of that new day. The early ancestors of modern humans (*Homo habilis*), in turn, emerged two million years ago, or at less than two minutes before midnight on that day. Nothing places human existence into context quite like this projected timeline.

Astrophysicists, archaeologists, and paleontologists, in their research into the origins of humankind, suggest this was neither "cosmically special" nor "unique"—maybe an "evolutionary accident."[22] Adding to the scientific understanding of the origins of human life, a significant group of physicists, climatologists, and others predicts that the universe is accelerating towards entropy or depletion (as codified in the principles of thermodynamics) and will eventually crash like a "wave crashing on the shore." They argue that the stars will dissipate, with their remnants falling into black holes, where they will evaporate (back) into a gruel of elementary particles—suggesting that from nothing we have come, and to nothing we will return.

Human Evolution

Charles Darwin and subsequent evolutionists have irreversibly exposed the limitations of the sacred texts of the Abrahamic faiths on the origins of life. The mystery nevertheless endures on how a lifeless or prebiotic planet could evolve into forms of life ranging from single-cell amoebas to

---

22. Carroll, *Big Picture*, 52; see also Van Huyssteen, *Alone in the World?*, 54–66.

hominids that include some of the greater apes to "modern" humans and their immediate ancestors.

This persuades many believers to reject a literal reading of humanity having a God-given mandate to procreate and subdue the earth—resulting in major ecological and related threats that predict an emergent sixth mass extinction on planet Earth. Ian McCullum, a naturalist and psychiatrist, argues that the disregard of this warning undermines our psychological well-being by separating us from the cycle of life of which we are a part.[23] Harold Bloom, drawing on shades of gnostic dualism, suggests that in so doing we isolate ourselves in a "cosmic dungeon," cut off from the creative energies of life.[24]

The story of evolution has been a slow, vacillating, and uneven process. Drawing on recent scientific molecular research, David Quammen addresses the intertwined nature of evolution through the transfer of genes that rejects the common image of a neatly pruned "tree of life."[25] Using a different metaphor, Steve Olson likens evolution to "clouds forming, merging and dissipating on a hot summer day" rather than the more popular image of the branches of a tree.[26] The merging of genera and species aside, scientists agree that the universe and planet Earth are part of an evolving process with human life developing from a long and treacherous journey that began with the particles of the emergence of single-celled aquatic entities from the primordial soup roughly 3.8 billion years ago. Multicellular life, including a plucky little fish that ventured beyond the ocean, evolved over the next billion years, to include the birth of mammals and the emergence of early primates between fifty and sixty million years ago, with advanced *Homo sapiens* commonly believed (with some dispute) to have emerged in Africa approximately two hundred thousand years ago. Evidence suggests that journeys north may have been attempted as early as one hundred thousand years ago from which *Homo neanderthalensis* evolved in Europe, while *Homo erectus* evolved further in the eastern parts of Asia. Returning to the "pruned tree" analogy, it is commonly perceived that the formative migration into the Middle East, Europe, and Asia happened approximately seventy thousand years ago.

23. McCullum, "Pulse of Protest."
24. Bloom, *Flight to Lucifer.*
25. Quammen, *Tangled Tree.*
26. Olson, *Mapping Human History,* 43.

In summary

- Approximately 6 to 7 million years ago the population of African apes split into two distinct species. One group evolved into modern chimpanzees. The other, through multiple generations, evolved into the *Homo* genus.

- A significant development in human evolution occurred in the bipedal **Australopithecine genus**, which is estimated to have emerged several million years later. *Australopithecus africanus* appeared between 3 and 2 million years ago at the interface between great apes and humans, having both apelike tendencies and human characteristics, with elementary tool-making capacities.

- *Homo habilis*, which had a slightly larger brain, humanlike anatomical and facial features, and a capacity to develop more advanced tools, emerged between 2 and 1.5 million years ago.

- *Homo erectus* overlapped with *Homo habilis*, dating back to between two million and four hundred thousand years ago, and became extinct between approximately one hundred thousand and fifty thousand years ago. Distinguished by a larger cranium and brain capacity, *Homo erectus* species were the first hominids to leave Africa, migrating into Europe approximately 1.8 million years ago and later into Southeast Asia.

- The most advanced group in the *Homo* genus, *Homo sapiens*, with advanced anatomical changes and cognitive abilities, evolved in East Africa approximately two hundred thousand years ago. They migrated into Eurasia between one hundred thousand and sixty thousand years ago. Recent mitochondrial DNA research shows that these *Homo sapiens* are the ancestors of all modern human beings.

- **Cro-Magnons and Neanderthals** evolved in Europe and the Middle East about five hundred thousand years ago and are commonly regarded as subspecies of *Homo sapiens*. All subspecies or archaic *Homo sapiens* had disappeared by approximately forty thousand years ago—leaving modern humans alone in the world.

The giant step forward in human evolution is severally ascribed to the emergence of bipedal apes, the increasing size of the brain, the development of language, discovery of fire, and the growth of agriculture. Each phase of evolution contributed to the origins of speculative thought, memory, imagination, and advanced levels of creativity, with larger apes and early humans sharing genetic memories, emotions, and instincts, whereas self-consciousness, abstract thought, imagination, and intellectual capacity are the particular attributes of *Homo sapiens*. This is attributed by neurologists to an increase in the size of the cranial capacity from an estimated 400–440 cubic centimeters in Australopithecine fossils to a capacity of approximately 1,260 cubic centimeters in *Homo sapiens* men and 1,130 cubic centimeters in *Homo sapiens* women. Equally important are the intricacies of approximately ninety billion neurons in the cerebral cortex and other parts of the *Homo sapiens* brain. These changes are attributed to changing dietary practices, the use of fire, social experience and cultural exposure, the use of tools, agricultural development, the domestication of animals, and more. The changes are seen to have included the development of language, beyond the grunts and sounds of lower animals, that later evolved into dialects and separate languages.[27] The creation of storytelling, in turn, played a major role in this process, with the lessons learned being passed on and further developed in subsequent generations.[28]

Cognitive Revolution and the Birth of Religion

Acknowledging the importance of the increase in the size of the human brain, Yuval Noah Harari discusses the importance of language, artistic skills, intergroup communication, and agricultural development that were enhanced by experimentation and exposure, which were at the heart of the cognitive revolution. These developments became entrenched in social belonging and stability, together with advanced forms of imagination, fictional ideas, and further speculation about the nature of the universe. Significantly, Harari also discusses the negative aspects of language and stories that became a source of gossip and shared grudge bearing, which resulted in aggressive warfare between bands of *Homo sapiens*. This, in turn, resulted in a growing need for material resources to fuel mental and physical activity. And that required further agricultural development and the far-reaching entrapment

27. Harari, *Sapiens*, 20–21.
28. Livio, *Why?*, 117–34.

of animals in the web of human greed. This Harari describes as evolution's "biggest fraud," resulting from the rape of the natural order and tribal warfare. This led to conflicts and ownership disputes, the domestication of some animals, the purging of others, and the genocide of Neanderthals and other rivals to *Homo sapiens'* dominance. Social contracts, bartering, and trading patterns followed, together (presumably) with intrigue and lies, which are a feature of survival in a competitive world.

The development of religion was apparently both gradual and exponential as a result of the growing confidence of *Homo sapiens*. The development of language and communication, together with archeological evidence of abstract forms of cave art and the capacity for abstract thought, distinguish *Homo sapiens* from earlier hominids. Van Huyssteen defines these developments as a "propensity to ask questions" about existence that conceivably later contributed to the emergence of early forms of religion.[29] Iain McGilchrist, analyzing the left and right hemispheres of the brain, argues that there is no "God spot" in the brain, while noting that (to our detriment) Western culture has increasingly come to be dominated by the left brain. This, he argues, limits our "perception of the 'other' and whatever it is that exists apart from ourselves." His research further shows that there is "an accumulation of evidence in favor of religious experience being more closely linked with the posterior 'non-dominant' [right] hemisphere."[30] Neuroscientists argue that this less holistic response by the human brain to "outside" stimulation was preceded by a more inclusive cerebral response to earlier cultures and thought processes. Projecting backwards, this is seen by some biological scientists as a conceivable nexus between early forms of cognitive inquiry and the artistic human imagination.

Paleoanthropologists suggest that this transition from the earlier great apes (*hominins*) to *Homo sapiens* is reflected in early cave art, within which they discern an emerging human capacity to explore the unknown dimensions of existence, seen in the patterns, crosshatch markings, and adaptations of familiar animals and human figures on cave walls and fragments of stone. They argue that these artefacts were arguably an integral part of human survival and food security rather than mere decoration. Entering a new phase of existence that took early humans beyond the habits of their predecessors, they explored new levels of survival that gave birth to agriculture and animal husbandry, which required favorable weather,

29. Van Huyssteen, *Alone in the World?*, 94.

30. McGilchrist, *Master and His Emissary*, 91–93; Trimble, *Soul of the Brain*.

rain, and animal fertility. Anthropologists and religious historians customarily regard this need as having given rise to belief in benevolent and fiendish spirits, as well as ancestral and spiritual beings, which could be induced to support their needs or be persuaded not to execute their wrath, which Harari argues preceded an "agricultural revolution." He cites the architectural ruins and artefacts discovered in the Gobekli Tepe structures in Turkey (traceable back to 9500 BCE), and at Stonehenge in England (dated to 2500 BCE), as evidence of early human (religious) endeavors to draw on supernatural powers.[31]

Integrated into the evolutionary process, this understanding of the birth of religion begins to acquire a measure of credence for marginalized and skeptical believers who embrace the insights of the biological sciences—which is a position that effectively enjoys the imprimatur of the pope. Speaking at the Pontifical Academy of Sciences, Pope Francis recently observed, "The Big Bang, which today we hold to be the origin of the world, does not contradict the intervention of the divine creator, but rather requires it."[32]

Identifying the gaps within the story of evolution, there are religious believers who argue that had the subatomic particles, atoms, and related dimensions of the big bang coalesced in a way other than they did, the universe and life as we know it would not exist. Splicing their belief into the biological account of creation, their argument is that our very existence is testimony to the existence of God.[33] The naturalist rejoinder is that the complexity of these interlocking particles, of chemical reactions—not to mention the impact of energy, matter, heat, and gravity on life—could have been an accident of time. In other words, evolution effectively takes the discussion of origins further than either Aristotle's projected invisible "unmoved mover" or classical Newtonian physics, which regards the universe as a vast, slowly-ticking mechanical reality ruled by causal principles. The outcome is that both religious-minded fundamentalists and amateur scientists and theologians frequently reduce belief in the Abrahamic God to a belief in a celestial engineer or a skilled geneticist![34]

31. Harari, *Sapiens*, 89, 211.

32. Withnall, "Pope Francis Declares Evolution and Big Bang Theory Are Real."

33. Carroll, *Big Picture*, 298–302, referencing the arguments of Alvin Plantinga and Huston Smith in their encounter with the National Association of Biology Teachers in the United States of America; see also Haught, *God after Darwin*.

34. Wallace, *Confronting Religious Denial of Science*, 35–36.

Scientific and theological connoisseurs continue to debate the gaps in quantum mechanics in relation to the origins of the universe. It is, however, unlikely that many people would ultimately be persuaded to be religious or not on the basis of this discussion. Existential experiences of religion ultimately go deeper to encompass a sense of meaning and dependence on a sense of divinity in creation and human destiny.

At stake is the extent to which our cognitive resources have the capacity to explain the origins and nature of planet Earth and the greater universe. Whether this ethic is attained through science or religion, the shape of ethics has both positive and negative consequences for individual and corporate behavior. Human beings have the capacity to control biomedical disease and to manage global warming, as well as to create nuclear weapons destroy the environment. Futurologists warn that "affective computing," or artificial intelligence, is potentially boundless, threatening to transcend the capacity of humanity to control its own future.[35] Each phase of human evolution—from the capacity to make elementary tools and use fire to the ability to spawn technical revolutions—is huge. The genie may just be out of the bottle!

Atoms and Stories

Thoughtful theology explores the origins and nature of life's deepest existential questions and the evolution of these questions in each new age and context. It involves the difficult task of exploring the human intent captured in ancient and sacred texts as well as in oral and written records of the time. Linked to this is the equally difficult task of translating these ideas into modern thought processes, which necessarily includes a working knowledge of the science of cosmology and evolution. Bluntly stated, the contribution of theology to public debate is dependent on its capacity to affirm the dialectic between textual analysis and the empathetic understanding of religious traditions on one hand and a willingness to wrestle with the changing questions embedded in the worldviews of each new age on the other.

Van Huyssteen argues that a viable dialogue between science and theology requires scientists to acknowledge that universal notions of rationality cannot be reduced to a modern scientific methodology. Theology, in turn, needs to relinquish the assumed privileged spiritual data preserved exclusively in sacred texts and traditions. A viable public

35. Yonck, *Heart of the Machine.*

theology can only be forged through multidisciplinary dialogue, reminding us of the complex epistemological issues involved in this dialogue.[36] This places a heavy burden on theologians to (re)interpret orthodox religious doctrine in a manner that makes sense in the marketplace of cosmic and evolutionary consciousness.

Diarmuid O'Murchu, an ordained priest and social psychologist in the Sacred Heart Missionary Order, insists that theologians have no realistic alternative to the latest scientific understandings of the universe, arguing theology is obliged to and capable of pursuing its trade in the modern world in relation to quantum theory and related scientific arguments. In *Quantum Theology* and *God in the Midst of Change,* he goes further than most theologians in explaining the core ingredients of theology in terms of quantum mechanics.[37] He suggests there is an affinity between his notion of quantum theology and the spirituality found in the meditations of early religious mystics, arguing that the dialogue between theology and science has a potential to mature into the "supreme wisdom of our age."[38] Few empirical naturalists and scientists may reject what they see as a projection of religious spirituality into quantum theory and related scientific discoveries. Lyall Watson, a biologist, explores the realm of the supernatural and "paranormal events" in relation to what he calls the "blank spots" and "soft edges" in scientific theory that account for human experiences that go beyond the natural or material world.[39] Going beyond the exploration of possible links or affinity between science and theology as undertaken by O'Murchu, Watson explores the phenomena of telepathy, reincarnation, and communication with the spirits of the dead. The fact that their books have reached bestseller lists suggests a greater level of human interest in spiritual experiences, extraphysical notions of all creation, and the possibility of paranormal events than many disciplined theologians or scientists may realize.

Carl Sagan wrote of an emotional need for people to explore what he understood to be the "pseudoscientific understandings" of populist imagination. He, at the same time, warned against the religious rhetoric that undermines the potential impact of scientific research on an inclusive,

36. Yonck, *Heart of the Machine,* 1–43, 308.

37. O'Murchu, *Quantum Theology;* O'Murchu, *God in the Midst of Change.*

38. O'Murchu, *Quantum Theology,* 181.

39. Watson, *Beyond Supernature.*

integrous pursuit of holistic truth.[40] The claims of O'Murchu and Watson, as provocative as they are, make the more restrained approach of Van Huyssteen and Carroll potentially more attractive to those proponents of the natural sciences and theology who are prepared to venture beyond the boundaries of their established disciplines. Van Huyssteen argues that a "transversal intersect" is required between the disciplines of evolutionary biology, palaeoanthropology, genetics, theology, physics, neuroscience, and neuropsychology to take the current debate on religion and science forward.[41] Sean Carroll, in turn, cautions against the "ontological elimina- tionism" in the sciences, arguing that there is more than one way of talking about the universe—distinguishing between a fundamental, microscopic cosmology and what he calls "emergent" or "effective" ontologies that ad- dress human values and the nature of a purposeful life.[42] John de Gruchy, in his *Confessions of a Christian Humanist*, provides an understanding of theology that addresses the modern challenges facing believers with a level of pastoral understanding that goes beyond most texts in the growing li- brary of books on science and religion.[43]

Carroll, writing as a prominent theoretical physicist, interestingly defines himself as a "poetic naturalist." He quotes Muriel Rukeyser and ac- knowledges that "the universe is made of stories, not atoms." In what he calls a "therapeutic word," addressed to nonphysicists, he encourages the sharing of multiple stories, myths, and reflections on life, urging poets, musicians, novelists, and others to share their perceptions and stories about the uni- verse and the origins of life. He suggests two provisos: the different stories and theories need to be "consistent with one another," and they need to be "compatible with modern physics."[44] The sciences, he argues, offer the most convincing and logical contemporary explanations of the universe.

Carroll's "therapeutic word" draws to mind the thought of Pierre Teilhard de Chardin, a philosopher and Jesuit priest (trained in paleon- tology and geology) who spoke of a projected "Omega Point" present in the cosmic mystery that will be summed up in what he calls the universal "*noosphere*" (from the Greek word for "mind") that transcends human

40. Sagan, *Dragons of Eden*, 247.

41. Van Huyssteen, *Alone in the World?*, 108, 314.

42. Carroll, *Big Picture*, 21.

43. De Gruchy, *Confessions of a Christian Humanist*.

44. Carroll, *Big Picture*, 19.

comprehension.[45] Process theologians Alfred North Whitehead, a philosopher-mathematician, and Charles Hartshorne, a philosopher-ornithologist, from their perspectives, speak of the dual transcendence of the divine presence in nature and human existence, as well as the unknown "beyond," arguing that God is uniquely other and universally present, present in silence, metaphor, analogy, and imaginative projection.[46]

An Eternal and Silent God

Human development, embracing culture, religion, science, and memory has evolved over at least two hundred thousand years. These are traditions comprising myths, anecdotes, and distant memories, rooted in the cultural, social, economic, and political priorities of each new age. These developments are frequently ascribed by critics to wars and land-grabbing by seafarers, explorers, missionaries, traders, soldiers, and settlers. The presence of ancient and precolonial religions suggests, however, that religious and cultural practices are primarily related to ordinary rather than to related cataclysmic events. They suggest cautious explanations of divine presence as symbolized in the "still small voice" heard by the prophet Elijah in the face of "earthquake and fire" and the dominance of the prophets of Baal. This existential voice is heard in different ways throughout the history of the world's great religions as well as in the secular quest for understanding at the height of national and global crises.

This voice is heard in the poetic and powerful words of Karl Barth, who affirmed his faith in God's providence in the wake of the slaughter of European Jews and others in a war-weary world. He echoed the words of Holocaust survivors such as Elie Wiesel, Primo Levi, and Richard Rubenstein, who pondered life within and beyond the Holocaust. Barth's confession was faith in a God who is the "Unknown One, eternal and silent."[47] This is more than a cry of desperation in the chaos of the times. It was a theology that looked deep into the human condition in search of a new level of hope and human coexistence.

45. Teilhard de Chardin, *Phenomenon of Man*.

46. See Cobb and Griffin, *Process Theology*.

47. Green, *Doxological Theology*, in which he captures the essence of Barth's theology in his commentary on the *Epistle to the Romans, The Word of God and the Word of Man*, and *Church Dogmatics* 111/3.

This genre of theology suggests similarities to a wordless spirituality that reaches into the silent unknown, captured in what the *Heart Sutra* of Buddhism refers to as emptiness and the nothingness of philosophical existentialism. In the Abrahamic faiths, God is ultimately an "unknown mystery" made known in metaphors and symbols that can realistically only be partially revealing, as will be discussed in subsequent chapters. The "stern warning" of Karen Armstrong is that sacred or religious metaphors and symbols can be no more than an expression of human frailty, in which we endow our own ideas with divine reality—sometimes to lethal effect![48]

The antidote to the theological captivity that comes from the fear of both science and free thought is a newfound openness to criticism, and, where necessary, theological discontent. As the empirical sciences continue to impact the consciousness of believers, and human biology and evolution are taught in imaginative ways in schools, contemporary religious belief could undergo significant change. This could result in the biggest paradigm shift in the history of religion. Positively done, this can provide new meaning to ancient doctrines of creation and the immanence of God. Indigenous religions in Africa and elsewhere have given expression to what is experienced as a spiritual presence through ancestors, *sangomas*, miracle workers, shamans, and priests. Karl Rahner wrote of the "within" forever yearning for connection to the "without"—which is essentially a "within." This suggests an innate human predisposition to live a fuller, more communal, inclusive, and complete life.[49]

Religious Memes

A major obstacle to historical inquiry is the multiple memes that shape tradition, including folktales and legends that are often reproduced in fanciful ways.[50] From a critical theological perspective, entrenched religious memes run the risk of reducing the notion of the divine in the Abrahamic texts to the superficial misconceptions of religious populism. Loosely speaking, these misconceptions are often described by sociologists as the "cultural equivalents" of genetic DNA. Dawkins, in *The Selfish Gene,* argues that human culture in recent times has emerged as a "new kind of replicator" or

48. Armstrong, *Case for God*, 321.

49. Rahner, *Hearers of the Word*, 16.

50. Dawkins, *Selfish Gene*; Dawkins, *God Delusion*. Also James, *Religion Virus*; Blackmore, *Meme Machine*; Richardson and Boyd, *Not By Genes Alone*.

meme, second only to biological genes, in shaping human consciousness.[51] This is captured in the title of Paul Richardson and Robert Boyd's book, *Not by Genes Alone*, which argues that memes include legends, folktales, popular adages, hearsay reports, what is understood to be traditional wisdom, "basic common sense," and the perpetuation of "lived experience" and historical memories. Whatever the primary bases for religion, the populist tenets of religious belief have acquired a social status that shapes the consciousness of believers and the perception of nonbelievers about religion.

In *The Religious Virus*, Craig James suggests that religious memes are not otherworldly or divinely disclosed truths. They are invented, learned, or constructed stories that are embedded in and shaped by the communities conveying the worldviews of ages past. Not unlike biological genes, they are replicated, sometimes in modified forms, in successive generations. These modifications could conceivably include transcription errors or manipulation by scribes, priests, or others to promote compliance or devotion among believers. This is commonly seen in the case of the Ten Commandments, which scholars interpret as the culmination of tried and tested moral codes, elevated to divine decree. James illustrates this process in relation to the core monotheistic belief of the Abrahamic faiths, which he traces back to the effectiveness of what he calls "the most useful, effective and advantageous" practice of the Israelites, who faced unprecedented geographical, cultural, and political challenges in their migration to the "promised land." In terms of the prevailing belief of the time, each clan and tribe had its own god. Given the victory of the Israelite tribes over other groups, Yahweh, the Israelite God, was seen to be mightier than the gods and idols of all others. This belief was in time elevated to a notion of the one and only God,[52] which became a dominant and self-perpetuating meme that mutated further into contemporary forms of political Zionism, often exploited in the God-talk of Jewish politics. It is a meme, appropriated by Christians and Muslims, which accounts for triumphalism in Christian and Islamic faiths as embedded in their sacred texts and traditions.

Beyond Literalism

Endeavors to reach beyond entrenched memes and religious mindsets in quest of the original or eternal meaning of sacred texts is an extremely

51. Dawkins, *Selfish Gene*, 192.
52. James, *Religion Virus*, 15–40.

difficult, if not impossible, task. As discussed in the chapters that follow, in Judaism, Christianity, and Islam the dominant ideas or orthodoxy of each generation are heavily influenced by the prevailing context and culture of the time—instead of the literal interpretation of texts written in the idiom of their own time. Dietrich Bonhoeffer, in his *Letters and Papers from Prison*, penned shortly before he was executed by the Nazis in 1945, warns believers against submission to every passing phase of theology such as the German nationalism of his time. This provoked his question concerning what Christianity means in a world that he saw as "approaching a completely religionless age" within which thoughtful people could in good conscience no longer be religious—because of the capture of the very notion of religion in Nazi propaganda.[53] His insights are directly applicable in the broader context of violence, often condoned in the name of the Abrahamic faiths. In Western secularism, cultural, racial, and gender bias is similarly present under a thin veneer of inclusivity. The task of theologians is to expose this subterfuge. In Armstrong's words, despite the mental and spiritual stress involved in this exposure, it enables us to discover liberating "capacities of mind and heart" that go beyond the constraints of fundamentalism.[54]

Central to the dialogue between theology and science is nevertheless the warning that neither science nor theology should surrender the core principles or raison d'être of its respective disciplines. The integrity of science is dependent on an uncompromising and detailed study of material and human reality. Thoughtful theological inquiry addresses the nature of reality in a broader sense, seeking a critical understanding and expression of the human experience within past and present history. For a viable dialogue between science and theology to occur, scientists need to be challenged to engage with theologians, artists, and social scientists who are critical of the constraints of Western existence and belief. Theologians need, in turn, to resist the temptation to speak too easily of transcendent or divine truth.

Western conceptual limitations are reflected in crisis situations in South Africa, Palestine, Myanmar, Kurdistan, the Arabian Peninsula, the broader Middle East, and other hotspots in the world, as well as in ecological and related crises facing the universe. This requires critical reflection on the nature of "ancient truths" in the Bible and Qur'an in the context of the worldview within which they were written. The primary source of the Abrahamic faiths is embedded in the legends, myths, and stories of antiquity

53. Bonhoeffer, *Letters and Papers from Prison*, 362.

54. Armstrong, *Case for God*, 8–9.

and the mutation of these sources through the millennia. The French post-modernist Paul Ricoeur suggests that metaphor and story are the outcomes of "a thought process that *precedes* the language process."[55] He coined the term "hermeneutical suspicion" to reappropriate the lived experience often lost in literalistic readings of sacred texts and conventional belief. His concern is to replace the denotative theory of interpretation with a theory of language that favours the "double meaning" of scripture. This requires the discernment of the metaphors and legends within the primary words of scripture, in relation to existential quest for meaning, requiring the believer to explore the primary teachings of religious beliefs and ethical systems in the light of science and modernity. It further subjects contemporary values and worldviews to the lessons embedded in ethical insights of the history of belief, with a focus on ethical primacy.

The security and identity of huge numbers of religious individuals are dependent on traditional interpretations of this awareness. This places an onus on religious institutions to persuade devout believers not to absolutize or rarefy their beliefs into a dogmatic confession or anthropomorphic construction that borders on idolatry. It is suggested in the chapters that follow on Judaism, Christianity, and Islam that the religious elite have throughout history promoted authoritarian control over dissidents, freethinkers, and heretics. Excluding themselves from control of religious institutionalism, deviants from this authority are apostatized—often with the direst consequences. The final chapter explores the future of these faiths in a rapidly changing, interconnected yet institutionally controlled world.

Stories Matter

The challenge of dialogue on the meaning of life, the different religious interpretations, and secular explanations of existence, and the interface between theology and science pose the question of how absolutely basic or purist any ontology needs to be or, for that matter, can be. Intellectual disciplines, religions, cultures, and people to a greater or lesser extent all seep into one another. Carroll, writing from a physicist's perspective, cautions his colleagues against the elimination of all metaphysical ideas that fail to conform to a basic scientific description of the universe. He argues that there is more than one way of talking about reality, stating that there is a difference between a basic microscopic scientific ontology that seeks to uncover the nature of

55. See Atkins, "Paul Ricoeur."

cosmology and life, and what he calls "emergent" or "effective" ontologies that address human values and the nature of a purposeful life. He suggests a holistic sense of truth is "a bit more slippery" and complex than anything that scientists have to offer.[56] Within this context he urges participants in dialogue to tell their stories of belonging and purpose in life, whether religious or secular. His concern is that without a sense of purpose and ethical pursuit, life collapses into sterile, unproductive futility.

Carl Sagan, ever the uncompromising rationalist, listed "the doctrine of [divine] creation" along with astrology, the Bermuda Triangle, human consciousness after death, and communication with the spirits of the dead, as manifestations of "anti-scientific irrationality" that is "demonstrably erroneous." He argued that humanity is no more than an ephemeral granular element in the universe—a "flash of luminescence in a great dark ocean." At the same time, he spent a great deal of his life teaching, filming a TV series, and speaking in public, seeking to communicate the wonder and mystery of the universe to a general audience.[57] He lived a life of ethical responsibility and caring for planet Earth and humanity. Ann Druyan, Sagan's wife, who shared his scientific views and was a coworker with him on his educational projects, observed at the time of his death: "I don't think I'll ever see Carl again. *But I saw him.*" She was convinced that Carl and her meeting was a factor of mere chance and beneficence in the vastness of space and the immensity of time.[58] Not all naturalists have the ethical tenacity to face life's finitude with the ethical responsibility of Sagan and Druyan, but neither do most erudite theologians and passionate believers. Sagan and Druyan dedicated themselves to search for cosmic truth in continuity with the early discoveries of Copernicus, Galileo, Newton, and others, which Druyan suggests is a "sacred commitment." Stating that neither she nor Carl (Sagan) had ever encountered a "single bit" of what they ever regarded as sacred, their "search" for scientific truth was every bit as passionate as that of a devout and fervent religious believer.[59]

An alternative response is captured in the words of Walt Whitman and reflects old-fashioned wisdom and tolerance that may yet be needed to save the world:

56. Carroll, *Big Picture*, 428–33.
57. Sagan, *Cosmos*; Sagan and Druyan, *Comet*.
58. Sagan and Druyan, *Comet*, 387–88.
59. Druyan, "Ann Druyan Talks About," 25; italics added.

This is what you shall do: Love the earth and sun and the animals
. . . argue not concerning God, have patience and indulgence
toward people, take off your hat to nothing known or unknown
or to any man or number of men, go freely with powerful un-
educated persons and with the young and with the mothers of
families . . . Dismiss whatever insults your own soul; and your
very flesh shall be a great poem and have the richest fluency not
only in its words but in silent lines.[60]

The more we delve into the "reality" of life and the responses of the
wise, the foolish, the young, the old, and the vulnerable, the more we are
confronted with the mystery of life that we dare not diminish with easy
answers to life's biggest questions. Many people fear uncertainty, resorting
to the memes of custom as a form of security. This is, perhaps, where institutional theologians get it so terribly wrong. In both science and theology
silence, in its different formats, is a tried and tested response to difficult
questions. The best theology deepens the ultimate questions of life rather
than providing trite answers to questions that neither theology nor science
have (yet) been able to fully answer. The journey is unknown, if not unknowable, captured in sacred texts as attitude and ethical behavior (rather
than epistemological speculation), which involves respect for the vastness
of the cosmic, dependence on the fragility of ecological reality, love for others, and humility before ultimate truth. Thoughtful spirituality is captured
in the haiku poetry of Peter Folb:[61]

The chance of life
Infinitesimally small
Purely accident?

Chances are remote
Seven hundred quintillion
Totally random
The chances of life
One in seventeen trillion
Just accidental

---

60. Whitman, "Preface to the 1855 second edition of *Leaves of Grass*."
61. Folb, *Raindrops are Falling* (Cape Town: Imagovisual, 2018), 4.

2

The Being of God

A little philosophy inclineth man's mind to atheism, but
depth in philosophy bringeth men's minds about to religion.

—*Francis Bacon*[1]

So, what precisely is theology? No longer the "queen of the sciences." More than a defence of an illusion, it is a useful irritant to both conceited believers and patronizing atheists. It is an open-ended model through which to ponder the universe—asking where humans fit into it.

Despite the monotheistic "conclusions" central to the Abrahamic faiths, Judaism, Christianity, and Islam are ultimately apophatic (ineffable) faiths, with scriptures cautioning against any attempt to name or describe God. Having endured successes and failures through a long and conflictual history, Judaism has as its focal point the affirmation of the unique transcendence of God. Institutional Christianity, with the support of Constantine l, effectively closed down internal debate concerning divine reality through the adoption of the Nicene Creed and subsequent proclamations. Islam unflinchingly affirmed the "wholly otherness" of Allah as written in the Qur'an, beyond comprehension, imagination, or definition. The three major Abrahamic faiths, however, for different reasons all drifted into a willingness to use their belief in God to support their survival and in aggression against their enemies. Judaism embraced the promise of the Abrahamic God though Zionism and in response to genocide. Christianity embraced the advantages of becoming a state

1. Bacon, *Essays, Civil and Moral.*

religion and underpinning Western civilization. Islam became embroiled in machinations of caliphate theology in the Arab world. These events are discussed in the chapters on these religions.

Theology necessarily does not provide a comprehensive answer to life's mysteries, nor does it assume to know or understand the nature of "ultimate reality." It is part of a wider interdisciplinary debate that seeks to contribute a set of open-ended perspectives on "ultimate reality" as reflected in the words and linguistic ambiguities of the Hebrew scriptures, the New Testament, and the Holy Qur'an, as well as in the art, architecture, ritual, philosophical debate, and historical inquiry related to these texts. Difficult to define in abstract terms, "ultimacy" is perhaps best recognized when seen both within formal theological debate and in the poetry, literature, and reflections of believers, nonbelievers, and secularists who are enthralled or antagonized by the beauty or tragedy of life.

No attempt is made here to identify the long and meandering debate on the "being of God" that extends back to the origins of *Homo sapiens*, as addressed in a number of important studies undertaken through different scholarly lenses.[2] This chapter provides no more than cross-references to aspects of these studies, with a focus on two important, sometimes neglected, provocations that have influenced the history of theological thought.

The one concerns the rationalism and rediscovery of Aristotelian metaphysics in twelfth-century Spain. Ibn Rushd, known in the West by his medieval Latin name, Averroes, produced a critique of dogmatic Islamic theology that inspired Rabbi Moses Maimonides and Saint Thomas Aquinas to review Judaism and Christianity through a similar lens. Despite the opposition to Ibn Rushd, Maimonides, and Aquinas from the guardians of orthodoxy in Judaism, Christianity, and Islam, these three figures subsequently left enduring influences on theological debate.

The other provocation came in the twentieth century from existentialism that reached its peak in the devastation of World War II. Existentialists argued that neither religion nor philosophical theory provides a satisfactory explanation for the absurdity of life. They insisted that it is the responsibility of each individual to work out life's meaning for him- or herself, by wrestling with existent cognitive ideas in relation to the emotive and intuitive feelings that are part of human consciousness. Jean-Paul Sartre argued in

2. In the addition to the recognized classics, more recent reader-friendly, comprehensive studies include Aslan, *God: A Human History*; Harari, *Sapiens*; Wright, *Evolution of God*.

a poignant sentence that "existence precedes essence," stressing that life is neither mentally nor spiritually predestined. Existentialists, popularly seen as angst-ridden, melancholic individuals (Sartre, Camus, Nietzsche, and others), often indulged in social excesses and frivolous activities, endeavoring to understand the contradictions of life in philosophical reflection on these and related activities. Despite Sartre's famous axiom that "hell is other people" in *No Exit,* he engaged extensively with people, enjoying a lasting relationship with Simone de Beauvoir, arguing that life is fulfilled in "not finding final answers" either in social excess or thoughtful withdrawal. Argued Sartre, life is devoid of any inherent, God-given purpose, so life's meaning can be discerned (if at all) only from *within* rather than in response to the contradictions of existence. In the words of William Butler Yeats, we are required repeatedly to "make and unmake" ourselves through the multifarious dimensions of life.[3] The importance of existentialism lies not in the conclusions reached by its proponents but in the insights inherent in the mutating uncertainties, fears, and absurdities of existence.

Debate on God in the West has been shaped over the centuries by classic Greek philosophy, metaphysics, ancient religions, mysticism, romanticism, atheism, and more. The major critics of established religion in this debate include Karl Marx, Ludwig Feuerbach, Friedrich Nietzsche, and Sigmund Freud—each of whom has left an indelible imprint on theological debate. Biologists, evolutionists, naturalists, natural scientists, and neurobiologists, writing in both scientific and popular publications, have made their own contribution to criticism of religious fundamentalism and have contributed to a more thoughtful debate on the existence or nonexistence of God.

Sam Keen suggests that an authentic quest for spiritual meaning and purpose in life—whether religious or secular—requires that we excavate through "layers of rubble, discarded beliefs, outworn creeds, broken hopes, shattered illusions and bones of flawed heroes" in traditional religions and beyond.[4] Scientists recognize that human existence involves more than a collection of atomic particles, general relativity, and quantum mechanics, while acknowledging the inability of science to explain this extra-empirical aspect of human existence.[5] The theological challenge is

3. Quoted in Oates, *Faith of a Writer,* 40.

4. Keen, *In the Absence of God,* 1.

5. Dawkins, *God Delusion,* 407.

to explore this "more" that believers recognize as a spiritual or metaphysical dimension of life.

This daunting task is partly captured in Rudolf Otto's emblematic reference to the *mysterium tremendum et fascinans*, or sense of *spiritual numinosity*, as an enduring reality in human life beyond rational explanation. Despite the caution of mystics and spiritual luminaries against the use of rash words in naming this mystery, populist evangelists and institutionally trapped rabbis, priests, pastors, and imams do precisely this. Rational, existential, and spiritual wake-up calls embedded in philosophy or religion have simultaneously kept alive insightful, courageous, defiant, and "heretical" thinking throughout history.

Fiction and nonfiction writers have directly and indirectly explored the enigmas and mysteries of life with more thoughtfulness than many religious and hard-line atheistic enthusiasts. Barbara Tuchman, in her *The March of Folly: From Troy to Vietnam*, cautiously refers to "ancient truths" as "a phenomenon noticeable throughout history, regardless of place and period," where society is confronted with a choice between life and death.[6] In her analysis of history, she suggests that human decision-making, wise and foolish, cannot easily be reduced to physical, political, or social factors alone. Refusing to offer any explanation for the enigmas of history, she lures her readers into pondering the nature of moral truths in the struggle for survival and dominance. Joyce Carol Oates, a leading contemporary American literary figure and humanist, discerns the deep need for meaning to be inherent to humanity. Written in a different genre from Tuchman's reflection, Oates's fiction and poetry, alongside her personal and critical essays, capture what she defines as "the human spirit yearning to transcend the merely finite and ephemeral to participate in something mysterious and communal called culture."[7] She argues that reflective people all question the anomalies of life, whether through creative thinking, speculation, myth, memory and storytelling, art, or music. This, she suggests, leaves the artist "born damned," needing to struggle through life with a sense of incompleteness, driven by a sense of inadequacy in pursuit of "complete redemption."[8]

Ironically, fiction, including the poetry of wisdom literature in primary sacred texts, is arguably closer to the scientific quest for the unresolved dimension of life than is the excessive trust in scientific method

6. Tuchman, *March of Folly*, 2–4.

7. Oates, *Faith of a Writer*, 94.

8. Oates, *Faith of a Writer*, 41.

(scientism) or in dogmatic theological belief. Metaphor, poetry, allusion, mythology, and story are increasingly seen as conduits between science and religion in contemporary debate.

Religion, Politics, and Science

Devout believers, conditioned by insular cultural and social environments, find it difficult to escape the conscious and subconscious comfort zones of their respective beliefs. This partly explains the spontaneous resistance to liberation and feminist theologies in fundamentalist religious circles. Max Weber reminds us that religion, like culture, is unlike a light cloak that one can cast off one's shoulders. It is part of our identity, formative experiences, unconscious impulses, and (memetic) memories instinctively imbibed in pursuit of life's purpose.

The nexus between religion, politics, and culture is addressed in the chapters that follow on Judaism, Christianity, and Islam. Despite the cozy, if not inevitable, link between these social realities, Judaism, Christianity, and Islam warn against the reduction and domestication of God to the demands of any particular time or place. In the Hebrew tradition, the name of G-d is understood as too sacred to mention. The New Testament reflects wide-ranging speculation by the closest disciples of Jesus, who struggled to understand the possibility of the humanity of the divine, and in Islam Allah is essentially seen as an incomparable, transcendent reality that cannot be reduced to human understanding. The high watermark of faith in the Abrahamic religions involves the praxis of love, peace, and justice measured in relation to the widow, the orphan, and the poor, rather than in rational understanding. Contemporary religious institutions frequently reduce this ethic to charity and almsgiving rather than a serious commitment to social change. The prevailing ideas in any institution are, as a rule, those of the elite and benefactors of that institution, who keep a wary eye on those who deviate from the principles embedded in a Constantinian-type synthesis of religion and state. This has resulted in theological support for tribal and nationalistic beliefs that are more prevalent and emotionally persuasive in religion than many devout believers care to admit.

Karen Armstrong poignantly warns that understanding of a "personalized deity" as portrayed in monotheism, has a tendency to slide into a notion of a protector-god of a particular group of people, shaped by race, gender, class, and culture.[9] The exposure of this malady is the defining characteristic of critical theology in feminist, Black, and other liberation theologies.

As I suggested earlier, twelfth-century rationalism, together with nineteenth- and twentieth-century existentialism, are among the primary theological tools that offer a self-correcting (and disturbing) dimension to religious complacency. Rationalism, in broad perspective, prioritizes the pursuit of truth that is often lost in the residue of anachronistic and dogmatic accretions in religion, as accentuated in the thought of Ibn Rushd, Maimonides, and Thomas Aquinas. Existentialism is both an extension and a critique of "pure" reason. It argues that the quest for truth requires an integrated and holistic response to life, which takes into account the emotions and personal anxieties that are overlooked in "pure" rationalism.

Twelfth-Century Renaissance

Rationalism was at the heart of the Golden Age of La Convivencia (coexistence) in Hispania between Jews, Christians, and Muslims. This period preceded the forced conversion and expulsion of Jews from Spain in 1492 and the expulsion of Muslims from Christian Spain in 1609, which thrust the three faiths back into the continuum of isolation and conflict. Critical historians argue that, apart from intellectual exchanges, the notion of religious tolerance at the time was essentially a misnomer. There are, nevertheless, indications of significant collaboration between Jews, Christians, and Muslims in art, architecture, literature, mathematics, science, and mysticism despite the tensions of the time.[10]

Details aside, the dialogue involving Rushd, Maimonides, and Aquinas had a lasting impact on the history of theological debate in the Abrahamic faiths. (A sometimes crusty old theology professor, at whose feet I once sat, and whom I continue to admire, liked to say: "These three wise men redeemed God from outer space, drawing Him back into human existence.")

Deeply involved in the philosophy debate of the time, the three addressed the devotional needs of traditional believers by drawing on the metaphors, parables, and storytelling of their sacred texts. Subsequent theological debate drifted between the dominant inflexibility of doctrinaire religious institutionalism on the one hand and the reaction of dissidents on

9. Armstrong, Case for God, 321.

10. Starr, God of Love, 211.

the other. The "three wise men" of the Middle Ages effectively spawned a new level of critique of orthodox notions of God as a Platonic man in the sky or divine engineer who controlled human destiny. Drawing on Aristotelian metaphysics, they revived a sense of divine presence in the natural order and history, discernible through rational inquiry.

All theology has a social context. The Visigoths who invaded the isolated Roman province of Hispania in 462 CE were, over the next hundred years, assimilated into the broader population consisting of nomad peasants, Berbers, Jewish and Christian refugees, settlers, deportees, and social outcasts. After their conversion to Christianity, Visigoth leaders were drawn into civic and ecclesial structures under the ambitious Isadore, archbishop of Seville (560–636), but rural peasants and marginalized communities were excluded from these structures. When these excluded groups were later recruited to resist the invasion by North African Muslims (Moors) in 711, they showed little commitment to doing so. The Moors occupied large sections of the Iberian Peninsula and established the efficient, independent Emirate of Córdoba under Abd al-Rahman I. He was the founder of the Al-Andalus (Muslim Iberia) dynasty, which ruled for close to three hundred years.

Christian leaders withdrew, forming an enclave along the northern border of Spain, where they licked their wounds and dreamed of regaining their former glory. Their alienation was compounded when Muslim invaders looked to local Jews, in preference to Christians (who were part of the old regime), to take responsibility for civic affairs. Córdoba flourished, experiencing economic prosperity and reconstruction that included the growth of library resources and the establishment of research centers that attracted Jewish, Christian, and Muslim scholars to the city. The Hindu-Arabic numeral system was introduced by mathematicians from the Middle East and elsewhere, and classical Greek manuscripts became available in Latin. Philosophy, the sciences, technology, medicine, art, and architecture flourished, with the Spanish reawakening impacting on the rest of Europe.[11]

At the forefront of this renaissance were the Islamic religious philosophers, Ibn Rushd (1126–1198), Abu Hamid al-Ghazali (c. 1058–1111), and others.[12] Rushd wrote treatises on medicine, astronomy, and physics, and produced commentaries on Plato and Aristotle. He, at the same time, revisited the history of internal debate within Islam on the nexus between philosophy and theology. Not least, his allegorical interpretations of the Qur'an brought

11. Lowney, *Vanished World*.

12. Rushd, *On the Meaning of Religion and Philosophy*. Further discussed in Chapter 5.

him into conflict with orthodox leaders in Baghdad, Cairo, and Damascus. Importantly, his dialectic between philosophy and religious faith energized the scholarship of both Maimonides (1135–1204) and Thomas Aquinas (1225–1274). This injected a critical voice into the dogmatic conservatism under the authority of an alliance between institutional religion and the political leaders in the broader medieval world, present to different degrees in Islamic dynasties, institutional rabbinic theology, and the resurgence of Catholicism in western Europe. These three wise men of the Middle Ages left their imprint on theology in the three Abrahamic faiths:

- *Ibn Rushd/Averroes* (1126–1198) contended that the pursuit of truth is humanity's highest good, arguing that the quest for the ultimate purpose of life was being undermined by the constraints of religious dogma. He reintroduced Greek philosophy into theological debate, raising questions that continue to influence progressive Islamic scholars today. He scrutinized Qur'anic and Hadith traditions, and in an apparent concession to the Islamic hierarchy, he allowed that there are two methods of truth-seeking in Islam: the one through the Qur'an, the other through philosophy and reason.[13]

He drew on the earlier philosophical teachings in Islam that reached back to Ali (600–661), the son-in-law of the Prophet Muhammad, the fourth "rightly guided" Caliph, and to Avicenna, also known as Ibn Sīnā (980–1037). Drawing on Aristotle, he insisted that essence (a pure idea) and existence (a particular or specific concept) could not be isolated from one another. This led him to examine natural sciences, medical discoveries, and prevailing notions of the natural and cosmic order as sources of pure or ultimate truth: If we follow the implications of medieval scholars about Ibn Rushd, we might hazard that were he alive today, Ibn Rushd conceivably would have explored the theory of general relativity and quantum mechanics.

For Rushd, truth was a single concept to be explored through all disciplines. Ibn Rushd was found guilty of apostasy and exiled by the *u'lama* for arguing that the Qur'an was either silent or ambiguous on issues that jurists had codified into law. Chris Lowney argues that the jurists effectively "shut the door" on intellectual *jihad* (struggle) in orthodox Islam, allowing them to deductively apply Islamic law in

13. Aslan, *Beyond Fundamentalism*, 155.

an authoritative way in the face of intellectual and related disputes.[14] He was partially exonerated after his death in the Berber city of Marrakesh (in present-day Morocco), and his body was taken to his home town of Córdoba for burial.

- *Maimonides* (1135–1204) came to be viewed by later generations as one of the most influential rabbis in medieval Judaism.[15] He prioritized the need to explain the complexity and deeper meaning of the Mishnah and Talmud to Jews who lacked the education to grasp the philosophical nature of his teaching. His publication of the *Mishneh Torah* (*Repetition of the Law*) included different rabbinic views on Sabbath observance, marriage rituals, prayer, and other aspects of Judaism.[16] His *Guide for the Perplexed* continues to be a tool for understanding the impact of ancient Greek philosophies on Judaism.[17] He was accused in some traditional rabbinic circles of violating Jewish law and misconstruing Jewish teaching through his allegorical interpretations of creation and other stories in the Hebrew Bible.

  The "Maimonides controversy" spread across Europe. Following the teaching of Averroes, he insisted that God's uniqueness meant God had qualities that "no other creature on earth possessed," arguing that humans can only know *that* God exists and *what* God *is not*. Embraced by many Jews, Maimonides's dispute with conservative rabbis, however, led him to withdraw from public debate and turn to meditation and silence, urging his followers to heed the words of Psalm 4 that counselled believers to "commune with [their] own heart upon [their] bed and be still." Maimonides was at the same time uncompromisingly consistent in arguing that there was direct continuity between rational thought and the spiritual practices of Judaism. Controversy aside, engraved on his tombstone are the words "From Moshe [Moses] to Moshe [Maimonides] there was none like Moshe."

14. Lowney, *Vanished World*, 170; see also Smock, "Special Report."

15. Maimonides's parents had fled Cordoba under fear of persecution when their son, Moses, was thirteen years old. He lived in Morocco and Egypt practicing as a rabbi, physician, and philosopher, influencing Jewish, Christian, and Islamic thought through his response to Averroes. He died in Egypt and is buried in Tiberius in present-day Israel.

16. Maimonides, *Mishneh Torah*. See also Gillis, *Reading Maimonides "Mishneh Torah."*

17. Maimonides, *Guide for the Perplexed.*

- **Thomas Aquinas** (1225–1274) came to be known as the father of Scholasticism. Like Rushd's and Maimonides's work, Aquinas's philosophical teaching and theology were influenced by Aristotle. In the aftermath of religious conflict and the crusades, medieval scholars remained largely detached from direct engagement in the political realities of the time, while Aquinas produced texts on the responsibility of kings and the oppression of tyrants in his pursuit of peace and social justice. He taught that "according to the natural order instituted by divine providence, material goods are provided for the satisfaction of human needs . . . Whatever a man has in superabundance is owed to the poor for their sustenance . . . The bread which you withhold belongs to the hungry; the clothing you shut away, to the naked; and the money you bury in the earth is the redemption and freedom of the penniless."[18] His major contribution was, however, as a catalyst for the growth of philosophical and critical thinking in European universities. Seen by some as the Christian Averroes, Aquinas examined the science and philosophy contributing directly to his natural law theology and to his understanding of the relationship between faith and reason.

Affirming the established belief that God is the unmoved mover and essence of creation, Aquinas taught that God can only by analogy be known through creation and meditation. Defining God as pure esse or existence, without form or composition, and the source of all creation, Aquinas simultaneously argued that the discernment of this essence is enhanced through thoughtfulness, silence, and in meditation. As did Averroes, Aquinas argued that there are two ways of coming to know God: Divina scientia and Sacra doctrina, with a higher, purer understanding of God coming through faith as taught in sacred doctrine and the devotion of the church. Aquinas's influence on Christianity was in many ways as subversive as that of Rushd and Maimonides. Pope John XXI instructed the bishops of Paris to investigate the complaints concerning the "heretical" use of Aristotelian thought in medieval Christian teaching and this resulted in over two hundred writings of Aquinas being restricted. These restrictions were, however, later annulled, and Aquinas became a growing influence in the church with his Commentaries on the Sentences of Peter Lombard, Summa

18. Bigongiari, ed., *Political Ideas of St. Thomas Aquinas*; see also Battenhouse, ed., *Companion to the Study of St. Augustine*; Thomas Aquinas, *Summa Theologica*, II,II, Article 7 (p. 171).

Contra Gentiles, and, notably, Summa Theologica being seen as the pinnacle of medieval Christian theology and philosophy.

Thomas Aquinas's affirmation of God not as *a being*, but *Being* itself, embedded in all creation and perfected in the person Christ, is addressed in the monumental works of Étienne Gilson and Karl Rahner among others, and has become a formative ingredient of Catholic theology and devotion.[19] The spirituality of Maimonides and Aquinas, as well as the broader mysticism of Jewish Kabbalism and Christian spirituality, was at the same time a parallel presence to the rationalism throughout the twelfth century and beyond.[20] Ibn 'Arabi took Sufi mysticism to new levels of popularity through the incorporation of women, peasants, and marginalized classes into Islam, with the influence of thirteenth-century Persian Sunni Muslim poet and Sufi mystic Jalāl ad-Dīn Muhammad Rūmī (simply recognized as Rumi) having reached well beyond the confines of Islam.

The influence of rationalists and mystics endures in the Abrahamic faiths. The rationalist debate on the ontological distinction between God and humanity was taken further in the nineteenth and twentieth centuries in Europe through the metaphysical thought of Baruch Spinoza, Gottfried Wilhelm Leibniz, G. W. F. Hegel, idealism, and the existentialists.

Nineteenth- and Twentieth-Century Existentialism

The metaphysics of rationalism and theological systems of thought came under new levels of scrutiny from late nineteenth- and then twentieth-century philosophical existentialists.

Both in anticipation of and in response to two world wars, existentialism captured the European intellectual turmoil and political despair of the time in its biting critique of religion, failed philosophies, and shattered

19. Gilson, *History of Christian Philosophy in the Middle Ages*, 406–7; Burke, *Reinterpreting Rahner*.

20. Spirituality acquired different forms in Protestantism, largely because of the tensions related to the *sola scriptura* debate that was central to the Protestant reformations. This contributed to the activism of Thomas Müntzer and other millenarians against the magisterial reformers, especially Martin Luther, who enjoyed the support of the German princes. Reacting to this activism, the magisterial reformers practiced a more controlled reading of Scripture and devotion that contrasted with the emotional spirituality and ecstasy among the radical reformers. Although differently practiced, this is arguably the basis of the current tensions between sections of the Christian Evangelical Right and mainline Protestants.

political "solutions." It offers "another look" at what Aldous Huxley called a "brave new world," within which the human quest for "true happiness" could be realized through medical science and technological development. To early and contemporary existentialists, Huxley's anticipation of an ideal world of happiness is an evasion of the harsh realities of existence in a world under the manipulation of religious and state institutions.

Søren Kierkegaard was seen as a proto-existentialist, his theology poetic and reflective rather than systematic. He rejected formal Christian doctrine, exploring the depths of anxiety and loneliness in "fear and trembling," arguing that "the awareness of spirit of truth can never be achieved but through despair," which involves the "dizziness of freedom."[21] Nietzsche saw religion as a source of mental asphyxiation, describing the church as a "snake" that needed to be throttled. In Friedrich Nietzsche's writings on the death of God, he asks whether the thought of God's absence was almost "too great for us to handle."[22] Albert Camus, a French-Algerian intellectual, rejected all prevailing beliefs and ideologies (including the "nothingness" of existentialism). In *The Myth of Sisyphus*, written at the height of World War II, in 1942, he proclaimed the total meaninglessness and absurdity of existence. Among the mid-twentieth-century existentialists, it was Jean-Paul Sartre who left the most lasting imprint on intellectual and theological thought. Sometimes he is seen to have inserted a "secular spirituality" into the existentialist quest for meaning in the face of his proclaimed sense of nothingness.[23]

- *Søren Kierkegaard* (1813–1855) completed his training for the priesthood in the Danish state church but refused ordination, arguing that each individual has to work out his or her own salvation and meaning in life, living as a "lonely individual in the crowd," who faces the barrage of life's choices. Arguing that Christian truth is neither more nor less dependable than any other option in life, he ironically took a "leap of faith" in which he embraced the mystery beyond the prescripts of Christian doctrine.[24]

21. Kierkegaard, *Fear and Trembling*.
22. Nietzsche, *Gay Science*, section 125.
23. Kirkpatrick, *Sartre and Theology*, 125–26.
24. Kierkegaard, *Attack upon "Christendom," 1854–1855*; Kierkegaard, *Concluding Unscientific Postscript*, chapter 2.

- *Friedrich Nietzsche* (1844–1900) argued that there no way of cogni-
  tively explaining the absurdity of human existence, stating he "breathed
  like one asphyxiated" under the imposition of bourgeois Christianity.
  Not only declaring that God is dead, he insisted that God needed to
  be killed, indeed "throttled like a snake" in order that humans might
  realize their full potential. Yet the equivocacy of Nietzsche's thought
  prevails. He places the words "God is dead" in the mouth of a "mad
  man" and asks whether the magnitude of the death of God is "perhaps
  too great for us to handle." He further intimates that the quest for life's
  meaning might be found in "the caves in which God's shadow may
  still be seen."[25] Pondering the state of Europe in his time and looking
  for a way out of political decay, he showed apparent sympathy for aspects of Nazism's clampdown on dissidence and chaos. These inclina-
  tions were seized on by Martin Heidegger and others who published
  synopses of his work in direct support of Hitler.

- *Albert Camus* (1913–1960) had a lasting impact on French and European society. In *The Outsider* (alternatively *The Stranger* or *The For-
  eigner*), he expressed his horror at societal indifference to the alienation
  of his native Algerians in French society. In *The Rebel* he reflected the
  existential depths of individual captivity to institutional control, while
  warning that the French Revolution had ended in tyranny.

  In *The Myth of Sisyphus*, Camus offers no alternative to the seeming
  pointlessness of life, captured in the absurdity of Sisyphus's task: to
  roll a rock up a mountain while facing the inevitability that before
  it reaches the top, it will roll back to the bottom. In A Happy Death,
  he talks of being open to "the sublime indifference of the universe,"
  recasting death not as something to be feared but as the only escape
  from life's drudgery.

- *Jean-Paul Sartre* (1905–1980), the most prominent of twentieth-century French existentialists, spoke of his difficult journey to atheism,
  with scholars questioning where the journey took him, discerning a
  "secular spirituality" in his rejection of religion. Sartre addressed the
  reality of collective captivity to institutional control, both secular and
  religious, from which he feared there was no escape. This is portrayed
  in *No Exit*, which involves the engagement between three culpable
  souls (Garcin, Inez, and Estelle) trapped in hell, unable to escape the

25. Nietzsche, *Gay Science.*

self-denial, guilt, and counteraccusations that characterized their lives. When the door of hell is finally opened, none of them is able to walk through it. There is no exit.[26]

Popularly seen as the promotion of societal melancholia and ennui, twentieth-century existentialism was a satirical quest for meaning that captured the interest of intellectuals, critical theologians, thoughtful believers, religious dissidents, and skeptics.[27] The absurdities of life are captured, inter alia, in parodies of Dostoevsky and Franz Kafka, who explore the cost of struggling for integrity and truth. In his remarkable novel *The Idiot,* Dostoevsky writes about a set of social ideals portrayed in the "positively good and beautiful man," Prince Myshkin, who is viewed by society as an idiot and a fool. Dostoevsky's rejection of the values of Russian aristocracy is a theme that underlies his classic novels *Crime and Punishment* and *The Brothers Karamazov.* Leo Tolstoy's *War and Peace* and *Anna Karenina* probe the reality of life through a similar lens, and Franz Kafka, a Bohemian Jew, allegorizes the stories of the Hebrew Bible and Yiddish folktales, creating literary symbols and bizarre images, challenging the absurdity of social convention.

The defining characteristic of existentialism is rebellion against the social herd instinct that holds individuals back from taking responsibility for their own lives by rejecting religious escapism, failed philosophical theories, and the political charades of their time. Existentialists argue that reason alone is insufficient to allay the anguish, anxiety, and dread that underlie human existence.[28] "Nothingness," a dominant word in existentialism, is a void pregnant with meaning in existentialist thought. Effectively it is a "house clearing" process that penetrates the ideologies and illusions of what Sartre called "lazy thinking."

Kate Kirkpatrick identifies a parallel between Barth's notion of "das Nichtige," involving the descent into the abyss of despair and the "nothingness" of existentialism. The difference is that Barth recognizes eternal grace as a source of delivery from despair to the possibility of new life. Similarly she sees Paul Tillich's notion of the "ground of Being," present in all creation and the God-given *essence* of life itself, as an alternative to the preoccupation of existentialism with the struggle for essence amid the tribulations

26. Sartre, *No Exit,* 1–46 (https://www.vanderbilt.edu/olli/class-materials/Jean-Paul_Sartre.pdf).

27. Kaufmann, *Existentialism from Dostoevsky to Sartre.*

28. Esslin, *Theatre of the Absurd,* 24.

of existence.[29] Describing Sartre as the "Socrates of nothingness," Tillich describes Sartre's relentless questioning of life as the primary challenge facing theology. For Barth and Tillich, humanity is faced with the stark choice between God's definitive "offer of life" and the collapse into nothingness in the form of "ontological nonbeing."[30]

Existentialist rejection of imposed institutional structures from dominant theologies has left a marked emphasis on Latin American, Third World, African, Black, and feminist liberation theologies. It is at the heart of Kairos theologies in South Africa and Palestine, which reject Western-based colonial and patriarchal theologies. The methodological point of departure in liberation theology is the struggle for conceptual freedom and inclusive justice. James Cone argues that each person and community must determine their own identity and well-being, as opposed to submitting to the prescribed classifications of others. He states: "In this sense Sartre is right, 'man is freedom', or better yet, man 'is condemned to be free'. A person is free when he accepts responsibility for his own acts and knows that they involve not merely himself but all men. No one can 'give' or 'help get' freedom in that sense."[31]

Drawing on the insights of existentialism, these theologies generate a corrective to formal doctrinal debate on life's enigmas and mysteries, insisting that individuals and communities ought to determine their own identity and purpose in life. This contradicts any suggestion that existentialism embraces a monolithic oeuvre, either for or against religion.[32] Broad-based existential methodology has become an ingredient within progressive theology that extends beyond a debate on the prescriptive limits of correct or incorrect doctrine.

This perception of religious belief from an existentialist perspective is potentially among the most damning and liberating dimensions of the history of religions. Scott Appleby suggests that we need to "imagine invisible quotation marks" around general terms such as *extremist, liberal, militant*, and even *religion* itself, in order to acknowledge the ambiguities in all

---

29. Tillich, *Courage to Be*, 140–50.

30. Kirkpatrick, *Sartre and Theology*, 139, 152. See also, Schüller, "Tillich's Life and Works."

31. Cone, *Black Theology and Black Power*, 28. Quoted in Kirkpatrick, *Sartre and Theology*, 196; See also Johnson, *She Who Is*.

32. Solomon, *Existentialism*, 1–2; Cooper, *Existentialism*; see also Wikipedia, "Existentialism" (https://en.wikipedia.org/wiki/Existentialism/).

beliefs.[33] Institutional religion, bolstered by social, cultural, and traditional (memetic and "authentic") memories, is being challenged as perhaps never before in modern history. Discerningly understood, no particular religion reflects a universal and timeless worldview. Understood from this perspective, existentialism has contributed to attracting the interest of a wide range of people who are seeking existential meaning, that exclusive doctrinaire religions fail to provide. Analogy and metaphor in relation to philosophical rationalism and existential philosophy are increasingly employed in mainstream religious commentary and especially in liberation and dissident theologies. Other Christian theologians, building on natural theologies and philosophical ontologies and ideas include the idealist philosopher, paleontologist, and Jesuit priest Pierre Teilhard de Chardin, and process theologians such as Alfred North Whitehead and Charles Hartshorne, who were at the forefront of merging theology and the natural sciences.

Everyday Reality

The struggle for meaning and human purpose inherent to existentialism and the dialectical theology of Karl Barth, Paul Tillich, and others has in more recent years come to be addressed in scientific and neurological debate on the nature of human consciousness. This is seen in discussion at the interface between science and progressive theology that explores the relationship between mental behavior on the one hand and the physical human brain on the other. Modern insights into the structure of the brain, which encompasses an infinite number of different connections between the nuclei and ganglia within the lobes of the brain's left and right hemispheres, lead to seemingly endless hypotheses concerning the physical brain and the abstract human mind. The left hemisphere of the brain is generally regarded by neurologists as the source of language, logic, critical thinking, science, and numbers, while emotions, music, color, images, face recognition, intuition, and imagination are attributed to the right hemisphere. An increasing number of neuroscientists prefer, however, to speak of the interface between the left and right lobes of the brain as the source of both rational and intuitive responses to the exigencies of life.[34] Iain McGilchrist argues that the smallest neuropsychological, anatomical, physiological, and

33. Appleby, *Ambivalence of the Sacred*, 15.
34. See Kluger, "This Is Your Brain on Creativity," 12.

chemical differences between the two hemispheres can potentially impact significantly on brain function and output.[35]

William Cavanaugh suggests that "Only those who are willing to face reality will discern mystery. And only those who are open to mystery will discover reality."[36] The concern of Cavanaugh and others is that while scientific methodology, involving the truths of mathematics and empirical research, provides crucial insights into reality, natural science, the social sciences, and religious tradition, it should not be allowed to lapse into triumphalism. We live in a complex world within which academic disciplines overlap. In a nuanced and holistic dialogue between science and religion it is the task of both scientists and theologians to keep each other open to ever-expanding intellectual and existential horizons. This requires both scientists and theologians to continually return to the drawing board, re-evaluating their hypotheses and verifications of the cosmos and what theologians refer to as the ultimate reality.

Scientists approach their work with uncompromising rationality, arguing that in the absence of empirical findings they are unable to acknowledge the divine or metaphysical reality. They further acknowledge that the scientific evidence of bouncing atoms and subatomic particles in cosmology is insufficient to explain the enigmas of human ingenuity and existence. Theology's failure to address these realities with similar candor undermines the possibility for dialogue and exchange between, on the one hand, the natural, biological neurological sciences, and, on the other hand, the social sciences and humanities—committed as they are to the study of the impact of social myths, human hunches, and common memories on the behavior of the majority of people in their everyday life.

Acknowledging the potential of neuroscience to eventually further understand the relationship between the physiology of the brain and the less tangible human mind, McGilchrist warns of the potential danger of neuroscience being able to manipulate parts of the brain to influence human behavior. He argues that while a purely scientific understanding of humanity fails to provide an adequate moral compass in life, the humanities and a nuanced study of religious traditions have much to contribute to protecting moral values so that they can adapt to meet future challenges.[37]

35. McGilchrist, *Master and His Emissary*, 3–7.

36. Cavanaugh, *Atheism & Scientism, Evolution & Christian Faith Project, Science & Worldviews*. Cited in de Gruchy, "Reality and Mystery," 59–70.

37. De Gruchy, *Led into Mystery*, 44.

Take away these guardrails on morality and Nietzsche's anticipation of chaos and the possibility of national and global dictatorships becomes a worrying possibility. In the last century alone the world has witnessed Nazism, fascism, apartheid, and genocides through the centuries. It could happen again in the current struggle for global hegemony.

Intellectual debate aside, the question is what institutional religion has done to counter the repeat of the ideological, political, and scientific factors that led to the conflagration of Europe in World War ll. In the Israeli–Palestinian conflict today, critical thinking on gender equity, racial equality, and political justice is marginalized or missing just as critical thought about Nazism and the looming Holocaust was absent in the 1930s.

Mark Jurgensmeyer's extensive survey of religiously inspired extremism and Karen Armstrong's *Fields of Blood* trace the intertwining of religion and political violence in theism as well as in nontheistic religions.[38] In the last century alone Jews, inspired by militant Zionists, have been at war with Arab states and Palestinians. They continue to militarily defend settlements in the West Bank and to blockade Gaza. Violence by Palestinian-based Fatah and Hamas extremists is defended by appeals to the Qur'an. Militant violence characterized Catholic and Protestant activism during the Troubles in Northern Ireland. Hindu extremism has been witnessed in the Indian Peninsula over the years, and Sikh militancy continues to be a source of conflict in the Punjab. The brutality of al Qaeda, the Islamic State, and related groups, and of the Taliban in Afghanistan and Pakistan, is perpetrated in the name of extremist jihadism. Violence in Burma/Myanmar is, in turn, perpetrated by Buddhist-inspired militants against Muslim Rohingya communities.

Violence by Christian Right and White extremists in America is said by the FBI to be the biggest security threat in the country.[39] Such violence often includes bombing abortion clinics, attacking people transgressing so-called normative sexual practices, and instilling fear through words and actions in communities of racial minorities. This extremism, often attributed to biblical prescripts by right-wing fundamentalist Christians, is part of the dark side of the continuum in what Scott Appleby calls the "ambivalence of the sacred."[40] His succinct interpretation of secularization illustrates the

38. Juergensmeyer, *Terror in the Mind of God*; Juergensmeyer, *Global Rebellion*; Armstrong, *Fields of Blood*.

39 Jones et al., "Escalating Terrorism Problem in the United States."

40. Appleby, *Ambivalence of the Sacred*.

shifts of the social location of religion from state control to civil society and organized religious enterprises that promote a variety of Christian beliefs and practices.[41] This ambivalence is reflected in overt and subliminal socio-psychological and religious levels, in the support of Western and American interests in the world as well as in the "rapprochement" between Vladimir Putin's government and the Russian Orthodox Church.[42]

The secret support for aspects of this agenda by sectors within mainline churches provides a fearful insight into the dark underbelly of Christian ideologies. Committed to the dominion of God over the private and public dimensions of society, they prepare for "cosmic war" between the forces of good and evil by drawing on isolated texts in the Hebrew Bible and the New Testament (attributed to Jesus or the apostle Paul) as justification for violence, without regard to the hermeneutical or editorial context within which these texts were written.[43]

Radicalization of Jewish, Christian, and Muslim religious extremists who passionately assume they are the agents of God in pursuit of regional or global redemption underlines the need to explore the depths of Abrahamic religion. Mainstream methodological hermeneutics requires that a particular text be interpreted in relation to the totality of scripture as well as the unfolding traditions in particular religions, and in Christianity and Islam in relation to creedal and jurisprudential statements. The history of the transmission of interpretations indicates a propensity to resist questioning institutional control. Trapped in and benefitting from these alliances, its own paternalistic structures of administration, the perpetuation of closed worldviews, and metaphysical constructs, and privilege, the institutional church is finding it extremely difficult to engage in the level of hermeneutical self-scrutiny needed to reestablish the familial bonds of the Abrahamic religious journey into an uncertain future.

The authoritarian contexts within which the "three wise men" and their associates in the twelfth century and existentialists of nineteenth- and twentieth-century Europe challenged the would-be intellectual and social oligarchs of their times and witnessed boldly to the capacity of vulnerable humans to reject the imposition of religious, state, and populist ideological control. The chapters that follow identify the importance of subjecting all intellectual edifices, whether in the form of sacred teaching or abstract

41. Appleby, *Ambivalence of the Sacred*, 4; 9.

42. See Ellis and Kolchyna, "Putin and the 'Triumph of Christianity' in Russia."

43 Juergensmeyer, *Global Rebellion*, 19–43.

ideas, to scrutiny and open debate. As we noted earlier, Nietzsche hinted at ultimacy "in the caves in which God's shadow *may still* be seen," and Barth spoke of God within "*das Nichtige.*" It's here that the quest for "ultimacy" amid the harshness of life's tragedies and the existential anxiety of individuals and communities, as well as the enduring dialogue between science and belief, will be pursued or shipwrecked.

3

Judaism: The Spirit of Prophecy

THE EARLY ISRAELITE FAITH, with its ancestry of polytheism, territorial and war gods, is the mother that gave birth to monotheism—the most powerful metaphysical force in Western civilization. Tracing its roots back to a covenant between God and Abraham some 3,800 years ago, Judaism has emerged as a distinct faith sustained by a subsequent commitment to the Ten Commandments, the love of neighbors, the welcoming of strangers, and the anticipation of a "promised land" within which peace and justice shall prevail. The challenge facing contemporary Judaism is to explain the implications of this belief within the context of the political and military power exercised by the State of Israel over indigenous Palestinians as well as its neighbors and strangers.

The history of the birth and origin of Zionism is long and checkered. Jews were expelled from among non-Jewish populations, as seen in the proliferation of segregated ghettoes and pogroms across Europe. Their only viable, yet perilous, escape was to renounce their identity, through assimilation into the dominant (Christian) culture of European nations. This inspired the notion of *Der Judenstaat* by Theodor Herzl through the establishment of the Zionist Organization, which would earn him the title of the spiritual father of the Jewish State. Herzl's dream gained support among alienated and landless Jews across Europe, not least as a result of the religious fervor of orthodox rabbi Abraham Kook, who drew on ancient passages in the Torah to support the belief that the Land of Israel was promised by Yahweh to the ancient Israelites and their descendants. Palestinians were driven off their ancestral farms. They rose up in resistance, and war broke out with neighboring Arab countries. This added a religious passion to a conflict that continues to fuel Jewish, Christian, and Muslim conflict in Middle Eastern and global politics.

Contemporary Judaism has come to be intertwined in the debate between political and religious Zionists as well as religious and secular Jews. Their different views are boldly portrayed in the multiple reviews of Ari Shavit's *My Promised Land: The Triumph and Tragedy of Israel*. Condemned by hard-line Zionists, praised by liberals, and criticized by anti-Zionists for not taking its analysis to its logical conclusion, the book is acclaimed by most independent observers of the Israeli–Palestinian conflict. Written against the background of eastern European genocide and the immigration of Jews to Israel, the book covers the violence of pre-1948 settler-Palestinian conflicts and the 1948 Arab-Israeli War (or Israeli Independence War). This is followed by an overview of the 1967 Six Day War and the Israeli occupation of East Jerusalem, the West Bank, the Gaza Strip, and the Golan Heights, as well as the building of permanent Jewish settlements in occupied territories. Next came the 1973 Yom Kippur War, the 1982 Lebanon War, and the Palestine Intifadas between 1987 and 2000.

Pivotal to Shavit's book is his argument that the Israeli occupation of neighboring territories and the building of permanent Jewish settlements was a crucial turning point from the ambiguities of the Jewish struggle for a homeland to the emergence of the State of Israel as a colonial power. He sees this development as undermining the continuity between the intent of early Zionism and the praxis of modern Israel, arguing that the modern State of Israel cannot be compared to ancient Israel, which comprised a remnant of the slaves from Egypt. Neither can the State of Israel be compared to the refugees of European ghettoes.[1] The Israeli–Palestinian conflict is, however, decidedly not resolved. The support of the United States and tacit collaboration of Saudi Arabia ensures the survival of the State of Israel. An important question is, however, whether the divided Israeli populace, not least the affluent and educated millennial class, is willing to embrace the self-sacrifice of earlier generations of Jewish settlers. Theological questions, in turn, include how long the religious elite in partnership with the current government can continue to successfully promote itself as the chosen people of Yahweh in an increasingly secular milieu. Alternatively, has Zionism been reduced to a civil religion or political myth, which contradicts a fundamental principle of Judaism and its sibling Abrahamic faiths involving the mystery of the Sacred Tetragrammaton

1. Shavit, *My Promised Land*, 201.

(the Being of God) as captured in four sacred consonants (YHWH)? For devout Jews the name of God is too holy to be spoken (Exodus 3:14). The eternal mystery of the divine surpasses human understanding and is beyond the reduction of God to political, ideological, or theological manipulation. Pious Jews, Christians, and Muslims regard this kind of parity as a blasphemous violation of the Sacred.

This spirituality is preserved in the Hasidic theology of the Polish-born rabbi Abraham Joshua Heschel, who insisted that while holy places "in space and in nature" are present in all religions, in Judaism "the idea of holiness gradually shifted from space to time, from the realm of nature to the realm of history, from things to events."[2] He provides a high watermark of monotheism and a prophetic corrective to the alliance of religion and politics in prevailing contemporary forms of Judaism, no less than in different manifestations of religion in Christianity and Islam.

Heschel's daughter, Susannah, captures the essence of her father's faith by observing, "Some religions build great cathedrals or temples, but Judaism constructs the Sabbath as architecture of time."[3] Whereas the ark of the covenant and the temple of David are celebrated in the Jewish faith as enduring symbols of God's presence in history, Heschel's theological accentuation of time is an iconoclastic rejection of any dogmatic, inert, or timeless interpretation of God's involvement in history. Heschel warns that at "certain moments the spirit of prophecy departed from Israel," contending that it takes a "special consciousness" and a "spiritual eye" to discern the presence of God in a changing world. This discernment persuaded him to participate in the civil rights march from Selma, Alabama, to the state capital of Montgomery in 1965: "I felt as though my legs were praying."[4]

The Jews, a tribe of desert nomads, staged a monotheistic revolution.[5] Rabbinic theology teaches that the *Shekinah*, or dwelling place of God, was exiled with the people after the destruction of the Second Temple in 70 CE and gave birth to diasporic Judaism, as well as to the emergence of the descendant religions of Christianity and Islam. Any spiritual continuity between these ancestral religions has been overshadowed by both anti-Semitism and

2. Heschel, *Sabbath*, 79, xiii, and 95.

3. Susannah Heschel, Introduction, xiii; see also Susannah Heschel, "Their Feet Were Praying."

4. Susannah Heschel, "Their Feet Were Praying." See also Susannah Heschel, Introduction.

5. Cahill, *Gifts of the Jews*.

neo-Zionist interpretations of *Shekinah* that sacralize the land in the form of the modern State of Israel. In celebrating the existence of the State of Israel, Heschel stated: "We do not worship the soil. The land of Israel without the God of Israel will be here today and gone tomorrow."[6]

Rabbi Jonathan Sacks, (an Orthodox Jew and former chief rabbi of the United Hebrew Congregations of the Commonwealth) draws on the Babylonian Talmud to warn against biblicism,[7] insisting there is "no text without interpretation" as a directive in his dialectic conversation between the Torah and worldly wisdom—that warns against the literalistic abuse of scripture while anticipating an emboldening to each new age to preside over the ultimate meaning of scripture and tradition to the ideological and political needs of each passing age.

Anti-Semitism

Milton Shain provides a deep and probing understanding of the historical context of anti-Semitism, describing Jews as the "classic other" in history, traceable back to Greco-Roman antiquity.[8] The Jews' resistance to religious and cultural assimilation was fueled by the early church's *Adversus Judaeos* writings, in which Jews were portrayed as the killers of Christ and as the antichrist. At a popular level, the "wandering Jew" was condemned to roam the world until the second coming of Christ and the Last Judgement. When Christians acquired an enhanced social standing in the wake of the Edict of Milan (313 CE) that followed the conversion of Constantine to Christianity, Jews were further marginalized in the Roman Empire and subsequently throughout the period of the Christian Crusades. This marginalization escalated further under Pope Innocent III when the Fourth Lateran Council in 1215 decreed that Jews and Muslims needed to be distinguishable by their dress as a basis for limiting social (and sexual) contact with Christians. Hostility toward Jews deepened in the wake of the expulsion of Jews and secret Jews (*Marranos* and *Conversos*) from Spain in 1492. This was followed by the expulsion of Muslim (*Moriscos*) converts to Christianity in 1609.[9] Significant groups of Jews migrated to Turkey, Italy, and North Africa. Others became unwelcome refugees across Europe.

6. Heschel, *Israel: An Echo of Eternity*, 120.

7. Sacks, *Great Partnership*, 252–54.

8. Shain, *Antisemitism*.

9. Majid, *We Are All Moors*.

Jews were personified in the devious and corrupt Shylock, immortalized in Shakespeare's *Merchant of Venice,* and seen as the nemesis of German purity in the folktales of the Grimm brothers.[10]

Eighteenth-century philosophers viewed religion as an anachronistic superstition and some identified Judaism specifically as a dangerous eccentricity that needed to be eliminated. Jewish persecution continued through the Napoleonic Wars (1803–1815) and the Russian pogroms that followed the death of Czar Alexander II in 1881. Seizing the opportunity when the Ottoman Empire lost its sovereignty to British and French occupying armies in the Middle East at the close of World War I, Zionists escalated their demand for an independent Jewish state in geographical continuity with the biblical monarchies of Judea and Israel, named by the Romans as Palestine.

Zionism

Theodor Herzl is commonly regarded as the father of secular Zionism. He actively encouraged the settlement of Jews in Palestine and became the first president of the World Zionist Organization in 1897. Twenty years later the Balfour Declaration, signed in 1917, proposed a "national home for the Jewish people." Promoted by Britain's foreign secretary Arthur Balfour, a Christian Zionist, and Lord Walter Rothschild, a leader of the British Jewish community, Jerusalem (which was part of the Ottoman Empire) was occupied by British and Allied troops six weeks later. It was, however, orthodox rabbi Abraham Kook who seized on this development to promote Zionism as a vehicle to persuade Jews to return to their homeland in fulfilment of God's promise of redemption of the chosen people of God. This created fertile ground within which religious and cultural Jews adopted a favorable attitude toward Zionism. Christian Zionists and premillennialists endorsed the return of Jews to the promised land as a prelude to the second coming of·Christ.

In anticipation of an independent homeland European Jews, fearing the intensification of anti-Semitism, sought refuge in Palestine without anticipating the complexities of post-Ottoman Middle Eastern politics. Tony Judt reminds us that the "imagined elective affinity" of Jewish migration ignores the ethnic mixing and political realities that have been an inherent

10. See Dundes, *Blood Libel Legend*; Shain, *Antisemitism*, 37.

part of Judaism since biblical times.[11] Younger Jews of diverse ethnic backgrounds had begun to discard the religion and culture of the ghetto and shtetl in the late nineteenth and early twentieth centuries, in quest of social emancipation and economic success. This resulted in clashes with incoming Jewish refugees seeking the comfort of traditional Jewish practices and was further intensified by the injection of British and French colonial self-interests into the Middle East at the close of the "Great War." A world-wide recession, the growth of European fascism, the outbreak of World War II, and the Holocaust also impacted on these developments.

In the wake of the eventual defeat of German and Axis forces, plus the media exposure of macabre pictures of the genocide, a new awareness of the extent of anti-Semitic theology in the Christian church began to be exposed. Anti-Semitism nevertheless endured, and some Christians refused to acknowledge Christian complicity in the genocide, giving way to a new awareness of Christian guilt, which ranged from the hand-wringing remorse of liberal Christians to the sober acknowledgement of guilt by others. New attention was given to the tireless and costly witness of Christian theologians (who included Dietrich Bonhoeffer, Martin Niemöller, Karl Barth, and others) while the silence of others in Germany and elsewhere prevailed. This included the refusal of Pope Pius XII to formally condemn the Nazis' genocidal slaughter of the Jews. At the same time theological "antisupersessionism" and Christian Zionism escalated, with the result that some Christians found their identity within the parameters of Judaism as a basis for proclaiming the imminent return of Jesus Christ as part of God's judgement on earth.

An important essay written by Daniel and Jonathan Boyarin in 1992 argues the roots of Zionism are essentially secular, political, and expansionist rather than religious. Writing in the wake of the 1992 Middle East Peace Conference in Washington DC, they warned against the dangers of the "human arrogation of power" that is entrenched in the notion of a "promised land." Drawing on the *Neturei Karta Statements* attributed to a splinter group of ultra-Orthodox Jews, they stated that the "labelling of the indigenous Palestinian population as enemies in order to sanction their (the State of Israel's) expansionist policies" is a "subversion of Rabbinic Judaism" that is "already boomeranging" against the State of Israel."[12] The Boyarins at the same time argued that the complicity of Christianity in anti-Semitism

11. Judt, *When the Facts Change*, 147–50.
12. Boyarin and Boyarin, "Diaspora."

is traceable to populist interpretation of Saint Paul's statement: "There is neither Jew nor Greek, there is neither slave nor free, there is neither male nor female. For you are all one in Christ Jesus" (Galatians 3:26–29). While recognizing Paul's commitment to inclusivity in the early church, it is important also to recognize that his theology mutated into what the Boyarins call a "genotype of sameness" in Christian liberal theology, to the neglect of cultural and changing contextual needs.

The critique of this "sameness" gave rise to the response of liberation theologians who identified the predominant, if subliminal, "whiteness" and "patriarchy" in liberal theology, which overlooks the unique experience of identity among Black, women, and poor believers. Their point of departure is that a liberal consciousness evades the experience of Black, women, and poor believers in theological construction. In so doing they focus on reading the Scriptures from the perspective of the poor and oppressed, drawing on the biblical record of God's redemption of the slaves from Egypt, the favoring of marginalized groups within and beyond Judaism, and the support of Jesus for women and victims of the established alliance between temple religion and Roman occupation forces in Jerusalem and Judea. A comparable alternative theology is present among Jews and scholars of Judaism, as manifest below in the writings of Marc Ellis, Walter Brueggemann, the Boyarins, Mark Braverman, and others. Their sharp distinction between political Zionism and a biblical understanding of Israelite history nevertheless continues to be opposed by institutional Judaism and Christian believers who support the State of Israel (in much the same way as liberation theology is largely rejected by institutional Christianity and Islam).[13]

The unqualified support for Zionism in institutional Judaism is seen most clearly in an article by Chief Rabbi Ephraim Mirvis, head of the United Hebrew Congregations of the Commonwealth, published in the *Telegraph* on 3 May 2016, in which he refused to distinguish between political Zionism and Judaism. He insists that Zionism is an "axiom of Jewish belief," the rejection of which he sees as an instance of "an ancient and insidious virus of anti-semitism."[14] Robert Cohen, a British-based Jewish critic of Zionism, responded by pointing out that Mirvis's utterances locate the 1947–49 invasions of Palestinian villages, the 1967 war, and the hostility of modern

13. Examples of the critique of mainstream Jewish and Islamic theologies: Marc Ellis, *Towards a Jewish Theology of Liberation*; Braverman, *Wall in Jerusalem*; Esak, *Qur'an, Liberation & Pluralism*.

14. Mirvis, "Ken Livingstone."

Israel toward Palestinians at the heart of Judaism. Cohen's commitment is to undo what he considers to be a theological and moral catastrophe for Judaism by creating a firewall between the Jewish faith tradition and the ideology of the modern State of Israel.[15] Significantly, Avraham Burg, a leading Israeli politician and businessman who shares Cohen's distress about the toxic impact of nationalism on the Jewish psyche and on Israeli society, argues that "Zionism is not a Torah. It's a chapter in our history. Let us move onto the next chapter."[16]

A hermeneutical principle that equates the biblical text with a dominant tradition poses the danger of potentially reducing crucial revelatory moments in the Abrahamic religions to state authority and public opinion. This is illustrated in the classic encounter of the prophet Samuel with the legendary kings, Saul, Solomon, and David, and is confirmed in the prophetic messages of Amos, Isaiah, Jeremiah, and others. Rabbi Jonathan Sacks, as I noted earlier, warns against "the bitter experience of factionalism" in Jewish history and the importance of theology remaining "open and accountable to the world," while providing theological support for the ideology of a "promised land."[17] Sacks's words point to the depth of an alliance between state and institutional Judaism that fails to take account of the bitter experience of history that prioritized national and tribal interests above shared existence that includes neighbors and strangers.

This message is frequently repeated in mainstream Christianity and Islam, which suggests the Achilles heel of the Abrahamic faiths is the temptation to align themselves with tribal, ethnic or national interests—effectively reducing monotheism to a tribal religion, which lapses into the justification of militarism. This is seen in the alliance of the early church with Constantinian imperialism initiated in the Edict of Milan (313 CE), the church's subsequent support for colonialism, Nazism, apartheid, and related forms of partisanship. It is similarly part of the crisis in Islam, rooted in Sunni and Shiite conflicts, caliphate ideology, and violent expression of jihadism as discussed in subsequent chapters. Acknowledging the dangers of sectional religion, the nationally aligned religion, Sacks warns that religious "sanctity should never be used as a shield against honest self-criticism,"[18] which arguably makes his

15. Cohen, "Thank You, Chief Rabbi."

16. Burg, *Holocaust Is Over*, in Braverman, *Fatal Embrace*, 63–74.

17. See Robert Cohen's response to Rabbi Sacks: Cohen, "Dear Rabbi Sacks." See also Cohen, "Sacks v. Corbyn."

18. Sacks, *Great Partnership*, 251.

theological "slippage" into political praxis both attractive to religious Zionists and the subject of criticism from progressive Jews.

Biblical Memory

Memory, tradition, and culturally infused religion, however, die hard. Central to Zionist thinking, from the religious fundamentalists to the secular adherents, is the assumption that history indicates an uninterrupted continuum from God's covenant with Abraham and his descendants to the modern State of Israel. David Ben Gurion, an avowed atheist, is reported to have said, "God does not exist, but he promised us the land." While this continuity is questioned by most scholars, it has become part of general belief, as portrayed in popular literature, on television, and by the film industry.

This history is seen to begin with an account of Abraham and Sarah leaving their home in Ur to become nomads. Their followers came to be referred to as 'Apiru (Habiru) or 'ibru, from which the English designation "Hebrew(s)" is derived. The meandering of Abraham, Isaac, and Jacob (renamed Israel) includes the account of Joseph, Jacob's youngest son, being sold by his brothers into slavery to traders en route to Egypt.[19] He was subsequently thrown into prison before being elevated to a senior position in the court of Pharaoh. Amid deception and intrigue between the brothers, Joseph arranges for his family to settle in Egypt. Their fortunes subsequently change, and they are enslaved, apparently with other Israelites. Scholars suggest it was during this time that the descendants of Abraham emerge as a nation with distinct customs, beliefs, and an identity. The foundational event of Israelite identity is the exodus or escape from slavery in Egypt under the leadership of Moses, and is remembered today in the Passover Seder, the ritualistic meal that commemorates Jewish delivery from slavery.

As the first five books of the Bible tell it, the Israelites travel through the wilderness for forty years before entering the land of Canaan, which they anticipate will be a "land of milk and honey." The Israelites claim it as "their" land. They are at the same time warned that this is ultimately "God's

19. The term *Israelites* is derived from the name given to Jacob, following his encounter with God in Bethel (Gen 35:10), and the name given to the "promised land" in Canaan occupied by the Israelite army under the command of Joshua. After the division between the Northern and Southern Kingdoms, the north retained the name Israel, while the southern kingdom took the name of its largest tribe Judah. When the Northern Kingdom fell to the Assyrians, the name Israel was again used to refer to all the descendants of Jacob. In 63 BCE the Romans occupied and named the territory the province of Judea.

land," and it needs to be honored and treated as such: "The land must not be sold in perpetuity, for the land is mine; you are strangers and sojourners with me" (Lev 25:23). The Israelites are to dedicate their first crops and to sacrifice their firstborn animals to God (Lev 27:30–33; Deut 14:22). To this was added the stern warning that should they become a proud and arrogant people as a result of economic wealth and power (Deut 8:7–17), they could face the collapse of their territorial and political dreams.

Canaan is shared between the twelve tribes of Israel that later merged to form a unified kingdom under the successive reigns of Saul, David, and Solomon before being divided into Northern and Southern Kingdoms. The Northern Kingdom is destroyed by the Assyrians in 722 BCE and the Southern Kingdom by the Babylonians, who carry the political and intellectual leaders of Israel into exile in 587 BCE. This results in a period of intense Jewish nationalism and restorationist belief, which endured until Babylon was destroyed by the Persians under Cyrus and the exiles were allowed to return home. Second Isaiah (chapters 40–55) heralds Cyrus as the anointed Messiah of God (Isa 45:1); and Third Isaiah (chapters 56–66) offers a reassuring message of God's favor: "For one brief moment I forsook you, but with great compassion I will gather you. In overflowing wrath for a moment I hid my face from you, but with everlasting love I will have compassion on you . . ." (Isa 54:7–8).[20] Jerusalem is again recognized as the City of David, and the covenant between God and ancient Israel is affirmed with new intensity. Ezra, a scribe and priest who returns from exile, located the Torah in the midst of the reconstruction process. Nehemiah, the "cup bearer" of the Persian king, who became the governor of Persian Judea, rebuilt the walls of Jerusalem to protect the ethnic and social integrity of the new state. The people of the "reconstructed nation" were seen as "the holy seed" and a "holy people." Ancient religious rituals were recovered and the foreign wives of returning Jews were deported to protect the propagation of the "holy seed" in future generations (Ezra 9:1–4; Neh 13:1–3).

Competing Traditions

Mitri Raheb offers a sobering comment in a situation where biblical texts are simply quoted against one another, without the context within which they

---

20. Isaiah is commonly regarded as written by different authors in different periods of history.

were written being taken into account. Not least with regards to the situation of Palestine, he insists there are "no innocent theological claims."[21]

The contexts of the intertwined traditions in popular readings of the biblical relationship between God and his chosen people are multiple.[22] This includes two covenants: The one involves the exclusivist and unconditional promise of God to Abraham, Jacob, and their descendants, where Israel is seen as the object of God's love, a people on whom God has set his heart (Deut 7:7–8; 10:15), the "apple of God's eye" (Ps 17:8), and the "holy seed" (Ezra 9:2; Isa 6:13) whom God will protect from alien influences. The other, articulated primarily in Leviticus and Deuteronomy, and drawn on by eighth- and seventh-century prophets, describes God's promise as being conditional on obedience to the Mosaic law (Gen 17:9; Lev 20:22–26; Deut 6:18; 28). This is a tradition that warns against ill-treating foreigners: "When a stranger sojourns with you in your land, you shall not do him wrong. The stranger who sojourns with you shall be to you as a native among you and you shall love him as yourself . . . [remember] you were strangers in the land of Egypt" (Lev 19:33–34). This is reinforced by the insistence that all land is God's land, which requires those who occupy the land to act as good tenants. For Brueggemann this is the "conditional *if*" in the covenant.[23] Mark Braverman's concern with Brueggemann's "conditionality statement" is that it effectively perpetuates the tribal favoring of Israel, which is used by Zionists and the State of Israel. They both contend that the formative Jewish commitment to the "love of neighbor" (that includes indigenous Palestinians) and the recognition of the rights of Arab nations is undermined by a hostile situation in the Middle East, despite the insistence of the Knesset that Israel is a Jewish State. Orthodox rabbi and Talmudist Joseph Ber Soloveitchik argues that "religion does not provide a solution to life's problem. Religion deepens the problem."[24] He insists that consistent with Jewish prophetic teaching, each generation must ask anew what constitutes justice and what must be done to promote peace in a given situation. Strategic and ethical analysis cannot capitulate to literalistic understandings of scripture without consideration of critical scholarship that explores the complexities of the transition between ancient Israel and the

21. Raheb, *Faith in the Face of the Empire*, 34.

22. See Horsley, ed., *In the Shadow of Empire*; Brueggemann, *Chosen?*, 30–36; Burge, *Whose Land? Whose Promise?*.

23. Brueggemann, *Chosen?*, 29.

24. Soloveitchik, "Sacred and Profane."

current State of Israel.[25] The literalistic use of scripture without regard to the gap between the time of writing and the context within which it is read is not only dishonest; it is analogous to the ploy of right-wing Christians to use ancient texts as a justification for the abuse of women and the aggression against people of other faiths.

Devotional reading of the scripture, no less so than scholarly interpretation of scripture, requires a careful analysis of past and present contexts to avoid the literal transposing of a biblical text into the contemporary situation. "It is clear," writes Brueggemann in a recent article, "that the Bible, as the rabbis have always understood, is filled with playful ambiguity and supple plural possibilities." The selective use of biblical texts inevitably flattens the ambiguity and subtlety of biblical history in its entirety, opening the door to the promotion of self-centered and tribal politics.[26] Robert Alter, professor of Hebrew and comparative literature at the University of California, Berkeley, defines Judaism as primarily a "culture of interpretation that refuses to be absolutized."[27]

Whose History?

Literalistic reading of scripture is exploited by ultraconservative religious groups, not least in the West, as a basis for the claim of uninterrupted continuity between ancient Israel and the modern State of Israel. Such reading leads to the implication that current-day Palestinians are no more than the possible descendants of a medley of forgotten peoples who once occupied Canaan. Mitri Raheb tells of an American woman, distressed by her visit to the West Bank, who said: "I don't understand why Israel is not adhering to the Bible. God told them very clearly to take care of the strangers." "That," suggests Raheb, "is exactly the problem! Who is the stranger?"[28] The Palestinians are not "strangers." They are natives of a land now occupied by Israel.

Raheb poses an important question: What happened to the ethnic groups and tribes that survived the invasion of Canaan by the Israelites, the establishment of the monarchy, and the successive occupations that

25. Finkelstein and Silberman, *Bible Unearthed*.

26. Brueggemann, "Reading the Bible amid the Israeli–Palestinian Conflict."

27. Kirsch, Review of *Ancient Israel*, by Robert Alter. See also Brueggemann, *Chosen?*, 36.

28. Raheb, *Faith in the Face of the Empire*, 37.

followed? These included major occupations by the Romans (63 BCE—313 CE), the Byzantines (326 CE), the Arabs (637 CE), the Crusaders (1099), the Mamluks (1291), the Tartars (1299–1300), the Ottomans (1516), the British (1917), and the Israelis (1948 and 1967).

As identified by archaeologists and historians in ancient inscriptions, artwork, and ancestral narratives, the religions of the *Am Haaretz*, the native "people of the land," changed through intermarriage, cultural assimilation, and evangelization by missionaries and traders. There was continual transformation of cultures and religions in the area. The meeting of the Christian Council of Jerusalem in 50 CE, for example, indicates the growth of a Christian presence in Palestine.

Whereas this history is largely overlooked in Western biblical memory, Palestinians trace their history through the storytelling of rurally based people in and beyond Palestine.[29] Palestinian Christians are writing theology from the perspective of their own grassroots experience that is in sharp contrast to a "church theology" that fails to recognize the occupation of Palestinian land by Israel. This is witnessed in the *Palestinian Kairos Document* and in the pioneering writings of Palestinians Naim Ateek, Elias Chacour, and others. Raheb's seminal work (in his latest book, *Faith in the Face of Empire*) develops this viewpoint further from a theological perspective. The historical work of Keith Whitelam (*The Invention of Ancient Israel: The Silencing of Palestinian History*[30]) and W. D. Davies (*The Gospel and the Land*) adds historical context largely overlooked in the West.[31]

Speaking at a conference on peacebuilding in the Middle East, Harvey Cox suggested that people get confused between the ancient Israel and the modern State of Israel; he argued that the concept of the "promised land" is being hijacked and abused for political purposes in the Middle East and stressed that the Israel referred to in the Bible and the modern State of Israel cannot be equated. "Therefore we have to be thoughtful and self-critical about how the theme is dealt with."[32] Walter Brueggemann, in turn, suggests, "The State of Israel, perhaps out of necessity, has opted to be a military power within global power politics," which distances it from the biblical record of early Judaism.[33] In stronger rhetoric, Mark Braverman points out

29. Raheb, *Faith in the Face of Empire*, 19–20.

30. Whitelam, *Invention of Ancient Israel*.

31. Davies, *Gospel and the Land*.

32. Cox, quoted in Brown, "Theologians warn."

33. Brueggemann, *Chosen?*, 38.

that "this image of the Jewish fighter, proud and strong, no longer the help-less, servile 'ghetto Jew', was and continues to be a dominant feature of the modern Zionist movement and a central theme in Israeli culture." This, he suggests, poses both the theological and the political question: "When did the image of a people redeemed from slavery and gathered at the foot of the mountain to receive the Ten Commandments morph into tanks rumbling over desert sands in a lightning war of conquest?"[34]

This distinction is often overlooked by the State of Israel and its allies in the West who draw on the history of anti-Semitism and the Holocaust to argue that Israel needs exceptional military protection and support. This runs counter to the accepted norms of political dispute resolution that re-quire honest negotiations, compromise, and a willingness to share a terri-tory with other people of that land.[35]

Post-Holocaust Theology

Understandably the reality of the Holocaust has become the dominant con-sciousness and identity of Jewish people, and the lens through which a large proportion of religious and nonreligious Jews understand the existence of the State of Israel.[36]

The impact of the Holocaust has produced legendary writings and re-flections by Jews whose names enjoy household recognition in the modern world. They reach the heart of religious self-consciousness and into the ten-sion between survival and belief. These writings explore what has become the defining question of post-Holocaust theology.[37]

Elie Wiesel, a Holocaust survivor, whose eloquent writings first helped bring awareness of the Nazi Holocaust to the attention of the wider world, recounts the gruesome memory of two Jewish adults and a young boy hanging on the gallows in Auschwitz. He writes of prisoners being marched past the hanging men and the boy. "The two adults were no longer alive. Their tongues swollen, blue-tinged. But the third rope was still moving; being so light, the child was still alive . . . For more than

34. Braverman, *Wall in Jerusalem,* 5; Also see Chernus's critique of "US opinion-shapers" in Chernus, "Three Myths of Israel's Insecurity."

35. See Chernus. *Monsters to Destroy.*

36. Herman, *Israelis and Jews,* 78–80, 203–13.

37. See Ellis, *Toward a Jewish Theology of Liberation*; Ellis, *Beyond Innocence and Redemption,* 7–46.

half an hour he stayed there, struggling between life and death, dying a slow and agonizing death. And we had to look him full in the face . . . Never shall I forget those moments which murdered my God and my soul and turned my dreams to dust." Unable to "describe the indescribable," Wiesel dedicated his life to communicating the tales of solitude, despair, silence, and defiance in the face of death.[38]

Richard Rubenstein's anger is expressed in his comment that the Holocaust happened not in small part because the collective majority of Jews complied with the demands of tyrannical regimes across two thousand years of anti-semitism.[39] He writes: "We learned in the crisis that we [Jews] are totally and nakedly alone, that we can expect neither support nor succour from God nor from our fellow creatures. Therefore, the world will forever remain a place of pain, suffering, alienation and ultimate defeat."[40]

Philosopher and rabbi Emil Fackenheim explores a middle ground between Wiesel and Rubenstein. He associates the Holocaust with Jewish abandonment of solidarity with other persecuted people, out of a desire for survival, while focusing on the "singularity of the Jewish experience, both in slaughter and survival." The Holocaust is for him a rupture like none other, including the Babylonian exile and the destruction of Jerusalem in 70 CE. It is in this situation, Fackenheim writes, that we are firstly commanded "to survive as Jews, lest the Jewish people perish . . . Secondly to remember in our very guts and bones the martyrs of the Holocaust . . . and thirdly [we are] forbidden to deny or despair of God, however much we may have to contend with Him or with belief in Him, lest Judaism perish. We are forbidden, finally, to despair in the world as the place which is to become the kingdom of God." Fackenheim warns against the use of past atrocities committed against Jews to condone the abuse of Palestinians and others by the State of Israel.[41]

Irving Greenberg focuses both on memory and on the obligation to create a new future for Judaism. He accuses Christianity, as well as liberalism and internationalism, of collusion in the Holocaust, asking poignantly whether one may "morally be a Christian" in the face of such complicity. He simultaneously warns Jews of the problems they face in state-creation and governance in the State of Israel. His commanding words summarize

38. Wiesel, *Night*, 44.

39. Rubenstein, *Cunning of History*, 68–77.

40. Rubenstein, *After Auschwitz*, 128–29; Rubenstein, *Cunning of History*, 68–77.

41. Fackenheim, *To Mend the World*, 213.

post-Holocaust theology: "After the Holocaust, no statement, theological or otherwise, should be made that is not credible in the presence of the burning children."[42] Drawing on the concept of *Tikkun Olam* (repairing the world), Greenberg states that the Jewish covenant with God requires them to set an example for the moral edification of humankind. Greenberg urges Jews and Christians alike to demonstrate an "openness and willingness to undergo the *ordeal of reorientation*" in their response to the Holocaust, which "closes out all [traditional] religious language." This reorientation requires us to "recreate the image of God" within the dialectic between the exodus as the promise of God's liberation and the Holocaust, while stressing the "infinite value, equality, uniqueness" of all people.[43] He remained loyal to the State of Israel until his death at ninety-one years of age in 2013, without his stated dream being realized.

A deeply empathic respondent to the reflections of Elie Wiesel and other Holocaust survivors, Robert McAfee Brown, a Christian leader in the fight against anti-Semitism, distinguishes between "Israel being [theologically] special" and Israel as a "normal" political entity, insisting that "as a state in warfare or dealing with refugees, it has to be judged like any other nation." Brown makes a plea to the Jewish people: "You, more than all other people on the earth, know what it is like to be refugees, sojourners, displaced persons, people whose lands have been overrun time and again by invaders . . . Could you not exercise the same kind of concern for the Palestinians 'within your gates' today?"[44]

Czech-born French writer Milan Kundera's words resonate in the context of the Israeli–Palestinian conflict: "The struggle of man against power," he argues, "is the struggle of memory against forgetting."[45] At the heart of the Israeli–Palestinian conflict is a clash of memories and the prioritizing of some memories to the detriment of others. Braverman argues that memory needs to include the post-Holocaust Jewish experience as well as the Palestinian experience "post-Nakba" (Arabic: "catastrophe"), which includes a loss of Palestinian territory, homes, and lives.[46]

---

42. Greenberg, "Cloud of Smoke, Pillar of Fire," 23; see Milligan, *Teaching in the Presence of Burning Children*.

43. Greenberg, "Cloud of Smoke, Pillar of Fire," 25.

44. Brown. "Christians in the West Must Confront the Middle East," 146.

45. Kundera, *Book of Laughter*.

46. Braverman, "Prophetic Theology for the Present Kairos."

* Selective memory is at the root of major conflicts throughout history. It feeds the presumption of the moral superiority of one's nation, tribe, or race as well as religious notions of God's special favor that often results in dire consequences for those who are not seen to enjoy this favor. This was seen in Nazi Germany's belief in Aryan superiority, in the Serbian cultural identity abused by Slobodan Milosevic to rally the support of Serbs in Kosovo in the late 1980s, in Afrikaner and colonial self-belief in White superiority in South Africa, and in the racial segregation policies of the United States. An underlying assumption in each of these scenarios was (and is) the right to social privilege, a responsibility to "manage" the affairs of others and an obligation to "police" regional and global politics.

The dialectic between the unconditional and conditional divine protection of Jews remains at the center of debate in the Israeli–Palestinian conflict. The unconditional assertion that the land belongs exclusively to Jews includes an epic narrative about early Israelites having spent 430 years as slaves in Egypt (Exod 12:40) and forty years in the wilderness, and the belief that the land was *promised, given, lost,* and *restored* in the State of Israel (Num 14:33). This assertion is at the heart of institutional Judaism, prevalent in populist Western perceptions of Jewish history, and supported by Western political interests in the Middle East.

Debate concerning the textual, oral, and traditional memories of ancient Judaism, subsequent forms of anti-Semitism, and the horrors of the Holocaust aside, individual Jews, Christians, communists, secularists, and atheists found a remarkable sense of common humanity in going to heroic lengths to resist Nazism in the darkest hours of the twentieth century. Resisters included Hannah Arendt, Berthold Brecht, Marc Chagall, Albert Einstein, Emil Fackenheim, Irving Greenberg, Abraham Heschel, Max Horkheimer, Primo Levi, Thomas Mann, Richard Rubenstein, Elie Wiesel, Simon Wiesenthal, and women in the *Sonderkommando* at Auschwitz-Birkenau and elsewhere, as well as Christian theologians and believers. The latter include Dietrich Bonhoeffer, Karl Barth, Paul Tillich, Robert McAffee Brown, and others.

The tensions within Judaism and concerning the promised land endure, while the prevailing politics in the State of Israel, as manifest in the Jewish-specific citizenship and identity enshrined in the Law of Return legislation passed by the Knesset in 1950, gives preference to Jewish immigrants entering Israel. This has resulted in the marginalization of native Bedouin Arabs, whose ancestors lived in the Negev for generations, and of East Jerusalem

Palestinians, whose citizenship in Israel has been disputed (at times revoked) since the occupation of the city in the 1967 Six-Day War.

Peace?

The Israeli–Palestinian conflict replicates the two dominant typologies of conflict described in the field of peace and conflict studies: *identity-based* conflict and *land-* or *resource-based* conflict.[47] This requires the acknowledgement of the reality of the past and the current situation facing Palestinians, as well as the past and present situation of Jews in the politics of Western involvement in the Middle East. The tragedy is that in religious, racial, and class-based conflicts, ranging from Algeria to Northern Ireland and South Africa, the patience of "nonpoliticized" victims of abuse lies dormant only until the fuse of revenge is ignited.

The Israeli occupation of Palestinian territory and Israel's resorting to military and security practices has inevitably resulted in Palestinians demanding the same rights for survival that Israel is claiming for itself. Irresistible force meets immovable resistance! The difference is that Israel is committed to territorial expansion and a form of ethnic cleansing whereas Palestinians are opposing Israeli occupation of their (Palestinian) land and the violation of their most basic rights. A "two-state solution" promoted by Western countries allows for neither secure borders nor economic viability for an envisioned Palestinian state, which will leave Palestinians vulnerable, insecure, and dependent on the goodwill and the self-interest of Israel, if not the whims and fancies of extremist Israeli citizens and settlers who continue to be granted the right to establish themselves on Palestinian land.

The task of biblical and theological scholars is to expose the misuse of the biblical narrative to support aggression by the current State of Israel, with the support of the United States, against the Palestinian people. Although biblical scholarship is often dismissed as a soft dimension in the world of realpolitik, the reality is that if and when a breakthrough comes in the Israeli–Palestinian situation, reconciliation and healing will be slow and fragile. In this situation, memory and critical theological thought could ease the journey toward transition and reconstruction.

Tony Judt argues that whatever the intent of the founders of Zionism, the occupation of land in the 1967 Six Day War and Jewish settlements in occupied territories leaves the State of Israel with three unattractive

47. Collier and Hoeffler, "Greed and Grievance in Civil War."

choices. One, it can dismantle its Jewish settlements and return to its pre-1967 borders, albeit with a dangerous and "constitutionally anomalous community of second-class Arab citizens." Two, it can pay the price of formally annexing its occupied territories of the Golan Heights, Samaria, Judea, and Gaza, whose Arab population, together with the Arab population in present–day Israel, will become a demographic majority within the foreseeable future. Three, it can maintain control of the occupied territories and face the hard reality of ethnic cleansing.[48] None of these options offers a viable solution in a situation where reality is overlaid with sacred memory. Politics, said to be the art of the possible, has failed after more than ten years since the Oslo Accords, signed in 1993 and 1995, and still supported by Israel and the United States. The realistic implementation of the Oslo "roadmap" to peace is at the same time being seen as increasingly impractical as the population in the Middle East increases and political tensions intensify.[49] Ari Shavit suggests that settler revolts, ultra-Orthodox revolts, resistance by an educated class of young people, the consequences of the 2006 Lebanon War, and subsequent threats from Hezbollah, Hamas, and Iran all point to the unfulfilled expectations of the Zionist dream and the vulnerability of the State of Israel. This, Shavit sees as resulting in an "existential challenge" to Israeli national stability, reflected in heightened tensions between opposition voices in the Knesset and civil society, ultra-right-wing parties, and the political survival of the Likud Party coalition. This, he concludes, raises questions concerning the difference between the will to resist among first generation and subsequent generations of Jews within the State of Israel and elsewhere in the West.[50]

Changing situations require ever-new strategies and strategic decision-making. This is the challenge confronting institutional Judaism, Christianity, and Islam in the face of escalating nationalism, increasing fragmentation, and rising economic inequality. The theological challenge reminds us that the Abrahamic God is an "itinerant God," who summoned Abram (later called Abraham) to leave his land, his gods, and traditions and to journey to an unknown land. Whatever is made of the origins, genealogy, and subsequent history of Jews, Christians, and Muslims, these faiths have imbued their histories and the interpretations thereof with sacred

48 Judt, *When the Facts Change*, 116.

49. The difficulties involved in establishing viable borders and a secure Palestinian state are discussed in Khalidi, *Brokers of Deceit*.

50. Shavit, *My Promised Land*, 328, 365–66.

status. Herein lies the problem: Ardent fundamentalists in these religions, with different levels of intensity, declare themselves to be God's chosen agents to impose God's will on earth. We must turn back to the mystery of monotheism's origins (the Sacred Tetragrammaton), who is holy Other, ultimately ineffable, and beyond manipulation of all political, ideological, or theological impositions. This requires an affirmation of the high watermark of monotheism in contemporary society, symbolized in the praying feet of Rabbi Heschel, in the civil rights march from Selma, Alabama, to the state capital of Montgomery in 1965, which captures the essence of prophetic witness from the Israelite and Abrahamic traditions.

4

Christianity: The Humanity of God

THE EMERGING CHURCH, DRIVEN by the will to survive, showed a measure of doctrinal reflexibility, openness to internal debate, and exploration of related and deviant beliefs. It adjusted to many of the customs, values, and demands in the diaspora, which resulted in the proliferation of different Christian sects and tendencies. This largely ended with the Council of Nicaea (325 CE) and ecclesial rapprochement with Constantine I. The church experienced a taste of socioeconomic and political influence, and the Christian elite molded the church into what would become the most authoritarian institution in the Roman Empire.

This phase of consolidation, however, never eliminated the process of internal debate or resistance to imposed hierarchical ideals or debate among Christians. Diametrically opposed forms of "truth" resulted in schisms, reforms, and the rejection of Christianity by scholars and former believers. Transcending denominational barriers, critical debate on biblical hermeneutics and on the validity of the established creeds undermines the authority once held by ecclesial synods, councils, and the church hierarchy—not least in liberal churches. Communal dispute and heresy charges are, in fact, often accepted by theologians and deviant believers as provocations for the church to rethink its sanctified version of truth and legitimacy concerning the greatness, invincibility, and immutability of God.

The reality is that there is little new under the theological sun. The proponents of each new era of theology trace the emerging changes back to the founding texts, myths, and oral traditions of Christian history. The history of the church nevertheless shows that the first ecumenical council in Nicaea was a watershed between the historic memories of Jesus' ministry and abstract projections of philosophical theology. The outcome of Nicaea was effectively the intensification of philosophical distinctions (in an effort to avoid conflict between the church and the state) to the neglect of the memory of ethical and political dimensions behind Jesus' ministry; the church in fact has relied on philosophical language to diminish the earthly significance of the gospel when such diminishment served the church's social interests.

Clearly, the flesh-and-blood stories of the life, ministry, death, and resurrection of Jesus of Nazareth in the four New Testament Gospels are different in genre, passion, and focus from the creedal theology of the church that has left a deep imprint on the institution itself. In a well-worn theological parody, the ascended Jesus, eager to catch up on the state of the church on earth, asks an archbishop who has recently arrived in heaven: "After all these years, who do people say that I am?" Quoting the authoritative Nicene Creed, the well-schooled archbishop confidently answers: "You are the one and only begotten Son of God, born of the Father before all ages, God from God, Light from Light, true God from true God, begotten not made." Jesus responds, "What?"

The foundational Nicene theology continues to influence Christianity. Convened by Constantine the Great (272–332), a despotic ruler with minimal knowledge of or interest in theology, the council was enjoined to eliminate the internal disputes that undermined the social cohesion of the empire. Traditional gods and the deification of emperors had failed to provide sufficient coexistence across an extensive and fragile empire, while the church, seeking to gain influence in imperial politics, made the necessary adjustments. This resulted in a theological abstraction that drew on classical (Greek) metaphysics to define as the Son of God a first-century flesh-and-blood Jew crucified by a Roman governor.

Distancing itself from its Judaic roots after the destruction of the temple and the flight into the diaspora, Christianity felt more and more the influence of Greek philosophy. The church soon spread beyond the Roman Empire and was exposed to African, Asian, and global cultural influences—and later to the European Enlightenment and the challenges of critical philosophy and science. All this exposure led to certain epoch-making events and schisms, in light of which, segments of the church had to go back to the drawing board, so to speak, in an attempt to rearticulate a mutating message, while continuing to be disturbed by the "dangerous memory" of the life of Jesus.[1] Christianity,

---

1. Metz, *Faith in History and Society*, 88–89.

like Judaism and Islam, has since its inception been subjected to different levels of critical thinking and reform—while being reluctant to face the full implications of the modern scientific revolution that disputes the veracity of Christian mythology. This anticipates a phase of internal theological and modern scientific debate discussed in Chapter 6.

From Jesus to the Christ of the Creeds

Christian history commonly starts with the narrative of cooperation between the Jewish community and the Roman occupation forces. Conquered by Pompey in 63 BCE, Herod was installed as "King of the Jews" in 40 BCE. The Jewish elite fulfilled its obligation to Rome through the office of the high priest and the Sanhedrin. These Jewish elites demanded tithes and exacted taxes from tenant peasant farmers in order to pay taxes to Rome and meet the costs of the temple infrastructure. At the same time, they collaborated with Roman troops to crush organized Jewish groups who rebelled against their subjugation. The Jewish population included the militant Zealots, Sicarii splinter groups, and ascetic members of the Essene and Qumran communities. The followers of John the Baptist and Jesus of Nazareth apparently distanced themselves from the violence of the Zealots and Sicarii, although evidence suggests affinity between these groups in terms of objectives.[2]

Resistance by Jewish rebel forces over time led to the destruction of the Second Temple and the razing of the city of Jerusalem in 70 CE.[3] Jews and

2. Smith, "Zealots and Sicarii."

3. Caesar Augustus, the first emperor of the Roman Empire, dispatched "Herod the Great" to be the client king of the Roman province of Judea in 27 BCE. Astutely balancing imperial interests with Jewish concerns, Herod's architectural projects included the rebuilding of the temple ("Herod's Temple") and the construction of his palaces and fortresses in Jerusalem, Masada, and elsewhere. He was succeeded by his youngest son, Herod Antipas. Less compromising than his father, he replaced members of the Sanhedrin with loyalists, crushed organized rebel groups and forced the high priest to offer sacrifices to Caesar Augustus as the Son of God. Jewish resistance escalated, and Rome decided to rule Judea directly by appointing Pontius Pilate as prefect in 26 CE. At the instigation of the high priest, Caiaphas, who reported that Jesus claimed to be the king of the Jews, Pilate ordered (perhaps as a routine responsibility) the crucifixion of Jesus. Governors came and went. Unable to curtail the uprisings of Jewish nationalists, Emperor Vespasian ordered his son, Titus, to crush Jewish revolts. Titus occupied Jerusalem in 70 CE, took the rebel leader, Simon bar Giora, captive and paraded him through the streets of Rome in chains, together with the sacred treasures of the temple. All of Judea was under Roman control except for Masada, the once-protected compound of Herod

Jewish Christians fled the city into the diaspora where they practiced their faiths in private ceremonies. Deprived of temple worship, Judaism underwent major revision. The character of rabbinic theology evolved as it encountered Greek philosophy and the allegorical Torah and Mishnah interpretations of Philo of Alexandria (20 BCE–40 CE). The impact of Hellenism, already present in the logos theology in the Gospel of John and the teaching of the apostle Paul, in turn developed further in the early church.

Mitri Raheb, however, importantly reminds us that Jesus was a Jew, born in the Roman-occupied province of Judea and exposed to the long history of conquest and the politics of regional Palestine. This included the memory of the united kingdom of Israel in the tenth century BCE and the kingdom of Judah in the ninth century, along with memories of the various conquests, by Assyrians, Babylonians, Persians, Greeks, and Romans.[4] This history and memory of conquest, Raheb suggests, partly explains the distinct theological paradigm of Palestinian Christians, who see resistance and liberation as the essence of the gospel, in contrast to the Western church, which draws on a later Anglo-Saxon and European period of history characterized by triumphalism and power.[5] Our beliefs are captured in stories, thinking patterns, education, architecture, music, and lifestyle. Imposed belief systems own us. It takes a concerted effort to think outside of a controlled social environment.

The account of Jesus and his crucifixion by the Roman procurator Pontius Pilate at the instigation of the Jewish high priest and Sanhedrin, at the core of the gospel records, is generally accepted as historically true. The wider account of Jesus' ministry, at the same time, reflects the influence of Jewish, Egyptian, Greek, and related myths, symbols, and memes.

Born between 6 and 4 BCE, Jesus was baptized at approximately the age of thirty by the Jewish firebrand John the Baptist and crucified by the Roman governor Pontius Pilate between 30 and 33 CE. A defining characteristic of the New Testament record is that Jesus' early followers struggled to understand who he was—a wandering preacher, a prescient messiah anticipating the end of history, John the Baptist, or a reincarnation of one of the Israelite prophets (Matt 16:13). Controversial in a deeply polarized

---

the Great, where a group of rebels took refuge until 73 CE when they took their own lives rather than surrender to Roman forces.

4. Raheb argues for "a new theological discourse." See Raheb, *Faith in the Face of Empire*, 40; Also Jenkins, *Next Christendom*.

5 See Raheb, *Faith in the Face of Empire*, 35.

society, Jesus criticized both the custodians of temple rituals and the vigilant oversight by the Roman authorities.

Only when read within the Palestinian and Middle Eastern context of the first century does the New Testament narrative begin to make sense, where Jesus is described as within the lineage of the legendary King David. The Gospel of Matthew quotes Jesus as saying, "I am sent only for the lost sheep of Israel" (Matt 10:6; 15:24), telling his disciples to go nowhere among the Gentiles and not to enter any Samaritan town (Matt 10:5). The anomaly is that in practice his ministry extended beyond the confines of prevailing Jewish customs and restrictions, as reported in his final command to his disciples to "go into all the world and make disciples of all the nations" (Matt 28:18–20).

Jesus was crucified as the "King of the Jews" (Mark 15:26) between two bandits, commonly understood to be guerrilla fighters or terrorists by the Roman occupation forces; this indicates that Jesus was seen as a seditious Jew. This perception required judicious management and elucidation by a fledgling church in the wake of his death. It took over two hundred years before political changes took place in the empire that allowed for rapprochement between Christians and institutional leaders in Rome. This rapprochement resulted in the Edict of Milan in 313 CE and the Council of Nicaea in 325 CE.

Carl Michalson speaks of the "double identity" of the person of Christ, which lapsed into a "paratactic heresy" (from the Greek *parataxis* meaning "to stand side by side, as in the line of battle") at Nicaea: according to Michalson, the council prioritized a "supra-historic" metaphysical theology over the historical act of God's revelation in Christ.[6] Writing in the 1950s, he argued that theology was not "deeply enough seized by its unique historiography." The danger of this development is the reduction of God's intervention in the life of Jesus to an "empty history," which contradicts the primary incarnational, flesh-and-blood dimension of New Testament Christology.[7] This cleavage, Michalson argues, undermines the Christian quest for meaning in history, and weakens the emphasis on Jesus' human life as the basis of Christian ethics.

---

6. Michalson, *Hinge of History*, 23, 35–36. He draws on the notion of "deficient syntax" to refer to the absence of conjunctions in language construction as an analogy for what implies a separation (if not a choice) between what is seen as a metaphysical theology and the historic act of God in Christ.

7. Michalson, *Hinge of History*, 23, 35–36.

Michalson speaks of a threefold Christology, consisting of the primary historic act of God in Jesus Christ; the spiritual confession of this act by believers; and a third step, involving the church's endeavor to understand the unity of the divine and human natures revealed in the life of the historical Jesus. Recognizing the Nicene Creed as a formative theological event in this third step, Michalson emphasizes the importance of recognizing that the mystery of God is ineffably beyond the finitude of rational human cognition, Greek metaphysics, and the niceties of Christian theology.

Marcus Borg's exegesis of the New Testament approaches this concern by reminding us that history is neither science nor art. He further argues that while historians cannot prove the identity of the person of Jesus, there is sufficient historical integrity in the New Testament narrative to recognize it involves more than psychological illusion or imagination. Borg reads the New Testament through the lens of a "historical-metaphorical" template, which suggests common ground between New Testament exegesis and the genre of historical novelists, poets, and investigative journalists who explore the social impact of people and events.[8] Borg encourages biblical scholars to explore the dialectic between the New Testament understanding of the person of Jesus and its relation to critical historical research.

The tendency to neglect this dialectic, and to harden the separation between the Christ of faith and the historical Jesus has emerged over the past two hundred years more by inference than design. The apostolic, Greek, and Latin fathers who directly and indirectly contributed to the pre-Nicene, Nicene, and post-Nicene Christology debate included among their number martyrs, social critics, church leaders, mystics, and scholars who withdrew into solitude and social exclusion, often to protest the excesses of the institutional church and society.[9]

Irenaeus (130–202 CE), the bishop of Lyon, sought to broaden Christian belief in individual salvation to include the redemption of all humanity and creation in a final act of *recapitulation* or *apokatastasis*, the end of the world (see Rom 8:21–28; 1 Cor 15:21–28; Eph 1:10). Origen of Alexandria (184–254 CE), in continuity with Paul and Irenaeus, suggested that as all humanity was impacted by the fall (dying "in Adam"),

8. Borg, *Meeting Jesus Again for the First Time.*

9. These included the apostolic fathers (Clement of Rome, Ignatius of Antioch, Polycarp, the Didache, and the Shepherd of Hermas), the Greek fathers (Irenaeus, Origen, Clement of Alexandria, Athanasius of Alexandria, John of Chrysostom, and the three Cappadocian fathers), and the Latin fathers (Tertullian, Cyprian of Carthage, Gregory the Great, Augustine of Hippo, Ambrose of Milan, and Jerome).

so humanity and all creation would be restored "in Christ." He argued that "not even the devil could escape God's redemption."[10] This belief in the redemption of all humanity and the entire creation is a dimension of early Christian teaching that over the years gave way to a prioritizing of personal, judicial, and substitutionary theories of salvation. The belief in the recapitulation of creation continued to be a feature of the theology of the Orthodox churches, although it was often forgotten by proselytizers and evangelical polemicists in the West.

The Council of Nicaea

Confronted by a number of different Christologies and doctrines of salvation, the Council of Nicaea faced the complex task of accounting for the historical and ethical origins of the Christian faith. Marcus Borg suggests that most of these traditions failed to demonstrate sufficient awareness of the essential historical and ethical origins of Christianity. Arians saw Jesus as the ultimate manifestation of humanity—a perfect human being, unreservedly human; the docetists, on the other hand, saw Jesus as the presence of God with an illusionary human body. Montanists, in turn, argued that the Holy Spirit continued to provide revelations from God that superseded those of Jesus, and gnostics believed that the knowledge of God was a universal possibility not dependent on Judaism or Christianity. Looking back at the political and philosophical milieu of the time, indications are that the christological debate shifted away from the historical, crucified Jesus toward metaphysical debate.

Referring to this tendency in the Nazi Christology in the twentieth-century German church, Johan Baptist Metz speaks of the "dangerous and neglected memory" of the humanity of Jesus.[11] Albert Nolan, writing at the height of the struggle against apartheid, laments in his formative publication *Jesus before Christianity* that "Jesus is a much underrated man [in Christian theology]. To deprive him of his humanity is to deprive him of his greatness."[12]

---

10. See Moore, "Origen of Alexandria."

11. Metz, *Faith in History and Society*, 88–89.

12. Nolan, *Jesus before Christianity*, 117. Nolan's concern became a formative influence in South African contextual theology in *The Kairos Document: A Challenge to the Church* in 1985.

This neglect can be traced back to the context of the Council of Nicaea, which ostensibly sought to promote a common belief concerning the person of Jesus. The knives were, however, already out before the Council assembled. The diocese of Alexandria favored a *logos* Christology (in which the *Logos*, or Word, takes the place of Jesus' human soul) whereas the diocese of Antioch favored an Arian, human Christ. The council was further divided by other anxieties in the broader church. These included imperial pressure to eliminate discord and social unrest in Christian communities. There were those within the church who were keen to gain acceptance and civic influence in the empire. Others incorporated customary cultural and gender differences in the emerging theology of the church. These included voices from believers who affirmed the revelation of God in all creation symbolically portrayed in the bodies of women.

This is powerfully captured in Sallie McFague's formative *The Body of God: An Ecological Theology*, which initiated a renewed emphasis on the intersection between humanity, the natural order, and the centrality of women in God's creation. For her part, Elizabeth Johnson suggests that the determination of the Nicene bishops to crush the Arians (who constituted the major opposition to their emerging power) resulted in their ignoring a deep-rooted feminine strand within Judeo-Christian tradition that experienced God in the likeness of a woman. Before the emergence of Christianity, this strand is visible in references to Sophia and "holy wisdom" in wisdom literature (Prov 9:1) and in comparisons between the quest for spiritual existence and a woman's laboring to give birth (Isa 42:14). Later the strand can be seen in the teaching and attitude of Jesus toward women.[13] A careful reading in feminist theology of the Hebrew and Christian scriptures further identifies the feminine motifs in the story of creation, masked in the patriarchal language of sacred texts. This is embraced and acknowledged in the history of women believers, this is acknowledged in the witness of nuns and scholars and formative contributors to the history of the church that include Saints Monica, Catherine of Siena, Joan of Arc, Teresa of Avila, and Teresa of Calcutta, as well as contemporary women social activists and theologians. Broad devotion to Mary the mother of Jesus is evident in the Roman Catholic and Orthodox Churches and more particularly in the heart of the tradition of Our Lady of Guadalupe in Mexico and the Americas.

13. Johnson, *She Who Is.*

An additional underlying critique of the Nicene Creed (by liberation theologians and others) is that while the creed acknowledges the crucifixion of Jesus Christ under the Roman governor Pontius Pilate, the Council of Nicaea failed to draw attention to the ethical implications of Jesus' resistance to the collaboration between the Sanhedrin and the occupation forces of the Roman Empire. Emerging from a period of perilous persecution, Nicaea prioritized the pacification of relations between church and empire while failing to affirm the ethical praxis embedded in the Nicene Creed. Seen from the perspective of Jewish atonement theology in the Hebrew Bible, concerning specifically the Day of Atonement (Lev 16; Isa 9) and the notion of the Suffering Servant (Isa 42:1–9), atonement is as much an act of social acknowledgement and a call to corporate transformation as it is a call for spiritual renewal. As the history of Christian praxis developed, this understanding of atonement morphed into personalized theories of judicial satisfaction and to penal substitutionary and related soteriologies. This led the churches to neglect the historical nature and reality of the crucifixion in the New Testament Gospels.

Effectively Nicaea left Christianity with what Carl Michalson calls an "empty history" that failed to communicate the passion and ethical praxis of Jesus and the early martyrs of the church.[14] This led to a symbiotic relationship between church and state that with few exceptions would determine the future history of the church in the West. Individuals and movements would from time to time rebel against this intimate relationship that is difficult (for either side) to walk away from. The selective memory of the New Testament account of the life and death of Jesus in populist images of Jesus, often supported by institutional churches, lends itself to many believers interpreting Jesus as little more than an abstract symbol of bourgeois complacency. Reinhold Niebuhr, a leading twentieth-century Protestant theologian, contrasts the life of Jesus, which he describes as an "impossible possibility," with both the dogmatism of the institutional church as well as contemporary forms of liberalism. An ethical realist and prominent critic of the Social Gospel movement, Niebuhr defines Christian integrity as including engagement in the tough socioeconomic and political decisions amid the changing demands of life. He advocates an ethic of "responsible living" that captures the overall intent of New Testament teaching but was

14. Michalson, *Hinge of History*, 23.

criticized for seeking to balance the "impossible" ideals of the Gospels with the complexities of modernity.[15]

Right or wrong in hindsight, Niebuhr refused to separate the abstraction of "correct belief" from the ethics of Christian decision-making. Ask a person what it means to be a Christian, and the chances are you will get a metaphysical response about recognizing Jesus as the Son of God rather than a response about the importance of the ethical values of Jesus translated into contemporary society.

The Nicene Christ is essentially an imperial Christ, a belief, based on a carefully constructed creed, couched in abstract language, distanced from the flesh-and-blood of Jesus of Nazareth. Greco-Roman culture had penetrated deep into the Roman Empire, and the categories of classical philosophy influenced every level of intellectual debate and the theology in the early church. The bishops at Nicaea were mentored in the pastoral tradition, ethical teaching, and martyrdom of Ignatius of Antioch, Polycarp, Saint Peter, Saint Paul, and others. Yet, when required to interpret the essence of Christian belief, they relied on abstract philosophical categories that devalued the cultural, ethnic, gender, and liturgical practices of other believers. This effectively gave rise to a paradigm in Christianity obsessed with tiny doctrinal differences that would bleed into a long history of dispute, fragmentation, and schism within the church. The doctrinal minutiae also gave a new incentive to monasticism (both within and beyond the institutional church), which focused on meditation, silence, and liturgy, as well as physical labor and charitable work, rather than on the philosophical preoccupations of the Nicene Fathers.

The triumvirate of politics, theology, and power that drove the Council of Nicaea was a lethal combination that changed the face of both the church and the empire. The Christ of Nicaea was the imperial Christ, and at Nicaea every attempt was made to focus on the unity between God the Father and Jesus the Son of God. This focus on the unity of God meant that church leaders relied on imperial and regional state institutions to defend the Nicene Creed and its social implications against theological deviants and heretics. One example of such a church leader was Augustine, who opposed the Donatist communities and the Pelagian heresy.

The definitive dispute was whether God the Father and the Son of God were of the same substance (*homoousia*) or of similar substance (*homoiousia*). Central to this debate was Arius, a dissident and influential

15. Niebuhr, "Relevance of an Impossible Ethical Idea."

priest influenced by Antiochene theology. He argued that Logos was created by God and was the first of all creatures, but not coeternal with God. Arius stated specifically, "There was a time when the Son [the Logos] was not." This was a position opposed to the dominant position of Alexander, the presiding bishop of Alexandria, who believed that Jesus was the eternal Logos of God. Refusing to submit to Alexander's authority, Arius doggedly persuaded Antiochene delegates in Nicaea to oppose the dominant position supported by the Alexandrian churches.

Arians saw Jesus as an exemplary and perfect human being who lived in total obedience to God—but not as divine. Arius argued that Jesus' divinity would contradict the very essence of monotheism. Athanasius, a deacon and assistant to Alexander, emerged as the formative voice in the debate. He galvanized the council delegates against Arius, which resulted in the definitive ruling of Nicaea that Jesus was the "Only Begotten Son of God . . . true God from true God, begotten not made, of the same substance as the Father."

Arius's teaching was declared heretical at the Council of Nicaea and he was sent into exile by the bishop of Alexandria. Still keen to unify the church in the wake of Arius's growing influence in parts of Africa and in some German states, Constantine later allowed him to return to the fold of the church. He died, either by poisoning or by other means, en route back to Alexandria in 337. His death gave new incentive to his followers to promote Arianism as an alternative to Nicene orthodoxy.

Athanasius was rewarded for his intervention in Nicaea by succeeding Alexander as bishop of Alexandria in an episcopate that lasted seventeen years. During this time, he recalcitrantly defended Nicene orthodoxy in a manner that earned him the wrath of his opponents, and he was sent into exile on five occasions by successive Roman emperors.

Nicene Creed

I believe in one God,
the Father almighty,
maker of heaven and earth,
of all things visible and invisible.
I believe in one Lord Jesus Christ,
the Only Begotten Son of God,

born of the Father before all ages.

God from God, Light from Light,

true God from true God,

begotten, not made, consubstantial with the Father;

through him all things were made.

For us men and for our salvation

he came down from heaven

and by the Holy Spirit was incarnate of the Virgin Mary,

and became man.

For our sake he was crucified under Pontius Pilate,

he suffered death and was buried,

and rose again on the third day

in accordance with the Scriptures.

He ascended into heaven

and is seated at the right hand of the Father.

He will come again in glory

to judge the living and the dead

and his kingdom will have no end.

I believe in the Holy Spirit, the Lord, the giver of life,

who proceeds from the Father and the Son,

who with the Father and the Son is adored and glorified,

who has spoken through the prophets.

I believe in one, holy, catholic and apostolic Church.

I confess one Baptism for the forgiveness of sins

and I look forward to the resurrection of the dead

and the life of the world to come. Amen.

As published by the United States Conference of Catholic Bishops. (http://www.usccb.org/beliefs-and-teachings/what-we-believe/)

The Post-Nicene Church

The post Nicene period of the church that followed the death of Constantine included the persecution of the church by Emperor Julian the Apostate, the consolidation of the Western Church by Augustine of Hippo, the fall of Rome, and events surrounding the Council of Chalcedon that would fuel the Great Schism.

Constantine died in 332 and the rule of his three sons threatened to undo the unity their father tried to achieve. Theological disputes escalated, Arianism prospered, and imperial support for the Nicene Creed wavered. This led to the short and intense rule of Julian (361–362), a nephew of Constantine who Christians designated Julian the Apostate. He reinstated traditional Roman religion in the empire, constrained the influence of bishops and priests, seized the assets of the church, and destroyed church buildings. This created a context for the slaughter of Christians. Julian was reportedly killed in battle against the Persians. With Julian's death, restoration of traditional Roman religion was essentially over. In its wake the church was left in disarray. Saints Jerome (345–420) and Augustine (345–430) restored unity and organization to the Western Church.

Augustine, Bishop of Hippo

Saint Augustine is best known for his *Confessions* and monumental *City of God*, but Augustinian theology continues to inform church-state relations in the West. Drawing on the work of the Cappadocian Fathers, he also wrote the formative *De Trinitate*, which established the Trinity as the basis of his theology. Negatively, he is also remembered for using theology to justify the use of imperial authority and military aggression to defend orthodox belief.

Born a proud Roman, Augustine justified cooperation between church and empire as pertinent to the welfare of the church. He argued that the "Earthly City" (the state) was exempt from the ethical principles of the "City of God," in order to impose earthly peace. He argued that the church was necessarily composed of both saints and sinners. Hence Christians were allowed to join the military to fight in "just wars" designed to preserve what he described as a tentative "Babylonian peace" in a chaotic and sinful world. This justified his belief in two separate but interrelated "cities" in the conflict between the empire and the Donatists, who traced their roots back to the Diocletian persecution between 303 and 305 BCE. Given that the Donatists found common cause with anti-establishment forces, including with peasants who attacked farmers, landed gentry, and political elites, Augustine called on the military to crush the Donatist rebellion.[16] In a similar manner, he condemned the teaching of Pelagius (350–425), who taught that humanity never lost its capacity to know and respond to God. For Augustine, this amounted to the rejection of the unique gift of salvation through Christ alone.

Augustine triumphed over dissent and heterodox views in the church—but at high moral cost to subsequent generations of Christians, who have drawn on his theology to justify their right to use military force against heretics and enemies. Rosemary Radford Ruether describes Augustine's theological justification for using state power and public sentiment to crush alienated peasants who were part of the Donatist uprising as a basic fault line in theology that has been perpetuated through social discrimination and violence that silences the poor, ethnic minorities, and women in the church.[17]

Augustine's political theology sans the excesses of history also, however, contributed to twentieth-century Christian realism, promoted by Reinhold Niebuhr and others during the Cold War. Countering the reluctance of liberal theologians to confront the forces of evil in the world, Niebuhr argued that it takes more than moral persuasion to combat social evil. Criticized for allowing American values to influence his "realism," Niebuhr also opposed religious intrusion into politics because of the danger of absolutizing political calculations. Employing this chastened Augustinian theology effectively in order to respond to life's exigencies requires careful political analysis and moral imagination as well as courage—all qualities on display in Dietrich Bonhoeffer's decision to participate in a plot to assassinate Adolf Hitler.[18] Chastened Augustinian theology also supports regulating religious extremism, whether Zionism, right-wing Christianity, or jihadist Islam, as I discuss in the final chapter.

Neither the Roman Empire nor Saint Augustine endured forever. The Vandals, a group of Germanic tribes who had converted to Arianism, invaded the city of Hippo and razed it. The control Augustine had exercised gave way to new conflicts in the church and to the emergence of Nestorius, patriarch of Constantinople and a "strongman" in the East.

16. See Lenski, "Imperial Legislation and the Donatist Controversy."

17. Beard, *SPQR*; Holland, *Rubicon*.

18. Niebuhr, *Moral Man and Immoral Society*; Niebuhr, *Why the Christian Church Is not Pacifist*.

The Council of Chalcedon

The church was part of a rough neighborhood within which the intrigue of theological belief often functioned as a cloak for hegemonic dominance in both church and empire. It was, once again, Antioch and Alexandria that evoked the major post-Nicene confrontation. As patriarch of Constantinople, Nestorius, a prominent member of the Antiochene school, reached beyond the formulations of both Nicaean and Arian Christology, contending that Jesus had "two natures and two persons." This came to a head when Nestorius rejected the established reference to Mary as the Mother of God (*Theotokos*), referring to her instead as the Mother of Christ (*Christotokos*). In response, Cyril of Alexandria, who emerged as the patriarch of Alexandria, (inevitably) responded by arguing that *Theotokos* preserved the perfect union of God and humanity in Christ (as Athanasius had affirmed in Nicaea).

This led to the Council of Ephesus, convened in 431 to resolve the dispute. After extended debate, the council condemned Nestorius's teaching, which resulted in his being deposed as patriarch of Constantinople. Despite this victory, the Alexandrian supporters of Cyril contended that the censure of Nestorius was too lenient. Cyril's backers insisted that Christ was at once God and human, which came to be known as *Miaphysite* belief. This was defined as a compound doctrine that defined Christ as a "unique being without separation, without mixture, confusion or alteration," and it effectively promoted a nondualistic consciousness within Christianity. Wanting to bolster their authority further, the Alexandrians called a second council in 449, which included more of their own supporters (and came to be known as the robbers' council). This further fueled the controversy between Alexandria and Antioch. Pope Leo XI sought to mediate, but his delegates were refused admission to the council, which collapsed into chaos.

Next came the Council of Chalcedon, in 451. It reaffirmed the Nicene Creed's emphasis on the hypostatic union between the two natures of Christ (human and divine), within whose humanity the majesty of the eternal God is revealed. The liturgy of the church was adjusted to include the Communion chant and further rituals in the Hagia Sophia, built by Byzantine emperor Justinian I in 538. The architecture of the church celebrated the "Holy Wisdom" seen in the person of Christ. Despite the careful wording of the Chalcedonian Definition, differing interpretations of delegates from the Western-based bishops in Rome and the Eastern-oriented bishops in

Byzantium or Constantinople (today's Istanbul) contributed directly to the subsequent Great Schism in 1054.[19]

The contours of discord that developed within the first five hundred years of the church, including in the wording of the Nicene Creed and the Chalcedonian Definition, continue to weigh on the identity of Christianity. The Nicene Creed was reflected on by historians, philosophers, dissident theologians, poets, and cynics.

The Chalcedonian Definition

We, then, following the holy Fathers, all with one consent, teach men to confess one and the same Son, our Lord Jesus Christ, the same perfect in Godhead and also perfect in manhood; truly God and truly man, of a reasonable soul and body; consubstantial with us according to the manhood; in all things like unto us, without sin; begotten before all ages of the Father according to the Godhead, and in these latter days, for us and for our salvation, born of the virgin Mary, the mother of God, according to the manhood; one and the same Christ, Son, Lord, Only-begotten, to be acknowledged in two natures, unconfusedly, unchangeably, indivisibly, inseparably; the distinction of natures being by no means taken away by the union, but rather the property of each nature being preserved, and concurring in one Person and one Subsistence, not parted or divided into two persons, but one and the same Son, and only begotten, God the Word, the Lord Jesus Christ, as the prophets from the beginning have declared concerning him, and the Lord Jesus Christ himself taught us, and the Creed of the holy Fathers has handed down to us.

As published in Theopedia. https://www.theopedia.com

The Great Schism

The divisions between the Augustinian church and splinter groups were precursors to further divisions, including the Great Schism between East and West. This involved culture, language, and aesthetics; imperial politics, papal extravagance, and ecclesial ambition. Theologically it included the

19. Dodds, *Pagan and Christian*; Hastings, ed., *World History of Christianity*; Wilkens, *First Thousand Years*; Irvin and Sunquist, *Earliest Christianity to 1453*.

iconoclasm controversy (not finally resolved until 787) as well as the *Filioque* declaration by Pope Leo I in 446, which stated that the Holy Spirit descended from "*the Father and the Son*," which formulation was rejected by the Byzantine leaders as an illicit insertion of words into the original Nicene Creed. Exacerbating these tensions was the crowning of Charlemagne on Christmas Day 800 by Pope Leo III (as the first emperor of the Holy Roman Empire since the fall of Rome in 410). Tensions escalated further, and in 1054 Pope Leo IX excommunicated the patriarch of Constantinople, Michael Cerularius, to which the patriarch responded by excommunicating the pope. This resulted in two separate churches. (The excommunications were not revoked until 1965, when Pope Paul VI and Patriarch Athenagoras I presided over ceremonies that lifted the decrees.)

The reemerging affinity between East and West reflects a cautious optimism for dealing with theological and intellectual deviations, beliefs, and doctrines, as well as heresy decrees in Christian history—all positions that had been hashed out in ecclesial and political hegemonic disputes, positions that had been defended by doctrines and rituals said to have come from God. A question is whether in the long term the church, and more importantly the world, is in a better place as a result of these bitter, alienating, and often arbitrary doctrinal decisions. In hindsight, probably not, but I return to this question in the final chapter. What is clear is that many of the declared heresies of the past have been resuscitated within the context of changing worldviews, both in intra-Christian and interreligious dialogue. Jerusalem and Athens have learned to coexist. Why not Antioch and Alexandria? Traces of Arianism are present in many liberal theologies, and Miaphysite notions of nondualistic reality are present in the progressive response of theology to the insights of the natural and biological sciences.

The Western Church

Subsequent to the fall of Rome in 410, significant groups of Christians left the city, becoming the nuclei of nascent Christian communities in Ireland, Scotland, the Netherlands, and Gaul (France). This contributed to the revitalization of the church in the West and the development of the Carolingian Renaissance in the late eighth century. The papacy grew in influence, and Pope Urban II (1042–1099) launched the Crusades against "heretics" and "infidels," which included an attack on the Muslim occupation of the Holy Land as well as on Muslim forces in Spain and parts of Italy, and on strongholds in the eastern parts of a once-integrated empire. The indiscriminate slaughter lasted for two centuries until the enthusiasm for Christian domination lost its spell. The church gained as much territory as it lost, prompting an inward shift toward spiritual renewal. Seeking future salvation, Christians undertook pilgrimages to Jerusalem for meditation and prayer. Theologians, in turn, explored a system of theology and philosophy through medieval universities and cathedrals that sought to reconcile the thought of ancient classical philosophers, not least Aristotle, with Christian theology. So scholasticism grew through the theology of Thomas Aquinas (1225–1274), Bonaventure (1211–1274) and Duns Scotus (1266–1308).

Scholastic theology essentially taught that *perfecta beatitude* is only attainable in the future life, while Aquinas in particular wrote on the responsibility of kings and the danger of tyrants in the pursuit of human peace and social responsibility embedded in natural law.[20] Like Augustine before him, Aquinas saw the church as an interregnum between an established political order and God's future kingdom, an expectation interrupted by the invasion and defeat of Constantinople by the Ottoman Empire in 1453.

Mercantile influences, which included the voyages of Columbus, sponsored by King Ferdinand II and Queen Isabella between 1492 and 1502, soon, however, drew Europe into the colonization of the Americas. The exploration of a sea route to the Orient, in turn, opened new opportunities for the church to spread its influence in the East, and the subsequent age of the Enlightenment in the seventeenth and eighteenth centuries. This period saw ancient philosophies and established forms of scholasticism, as well as popular superstitions and religious expectations, questioned by primacy of reason in the teaching of Descartes, Locke, Newton, Kant, Goethe, Voltaire, Rousseau, and others.

The Eastern Church

When Constantinople fell to the Ottoman Empire in 1453, the Eastern part of the church survived in deference to Mehmed the Conqueror, sultan of the conquered territory, who converted the historic Hagia Sophia and Parthenon basilicas into mosques, while allowing Christians to worship

---

20. Thomas Aquinas, *Summa Theologica*, II,II, article 7 (p. 171); Bigongiari, ed., *Political Ideas of St. Thomas Aquinas*; Battenhouse, ed., *Companion to the Study of St. Augustine*.

in other churches, with the proviso that they refrain from proselytizing or disrupting the Muslim social order.

By this time, the Oriental Orthodox Churches (Ethiopian, Coptic, Armenian, Syrian, Indian, and Eritrean), not to be confused with Greek or Eastern Orthodox Churches, had adopted a Miaphysite Christology, advocated by Cyril of Alexandria, which they prefer to define as "non-Chalcedonian" Christology because it opposes the theology of Christ's two natures, stated in the Chalcedonian Definition of 451.

The Eastern Orthodox Church prospered in Russia and was absorbed into the state bureaucracy by Emperor Peter I in 1721. Two hundred years later the Bolshevik Revolution overthrew church-state cooperation, with the church being cast as an enemy of the revolution. Czar Nicholas II and his family were killed, hundreds of bishops and priests were executed, and others fled the country as the Union of Soviet Socialist Republics (USSR), established in 1922, promoted atheism as a unifying strategy. Except for a brief period when Joseph Stalin sought to revive the Russian Orthodox Church as part of an effort to promote patriotism in the war against Nazi Germany, the church's priority was simply to survive—building its identity around the centrality of worship as the mystic union between Christ and his church. The Eastern Orthodox churches operated on what came to be called a principle of synergy or a middle way between the strict separation of church and state on the one hand and the fusion of the two on the other. At best, this principle influenced the church to be in "realistic dissidence" with the state, arguing that the kingdom of God would not dawn within human history. In brief, the Soviet state waited for religion to wither away, while the church anticipated a kingdom yet to be born.

Sixteenth-Century Reformations

Speaking out against papal supremacy, ecclesial excesses, purgatory, and the sale of indulgences, Martin Luther (1483–1546) accused the Roman Catholic Church of holding Christians "captive from the cradle to the grave."[21] This resulted in some affinity between Protestantism and the Eastern Orthodox churches (opposition to Catholic Church dogma), while Luther's focus on *sola scriptura* as the bedrock of the gospel started two different theological trajectories.[22]

21. Luther, *Works of Martin Luther*, 2:179–85, 186–87.

22. See Mastrantonis, *Augsburg and Constantinople*; see also Fenton, "Early Lutheran

Magisterial Protestant Reformation

The Protestant Reformation developed in relation to the critical thought of Desiderius Erasmus of Rotterdam (1466–1536), who condemned the abuses of the Roman Catholic Church. He saw Martin Luther as "a mighty trumpet of gospel truth," but later opposed both Luther's rejection of human free will and his call on the princes to suppress the rebellious peasants: Luther described the peasants in fact as "murderous, thieving, hordes," and insisted that it was the duty of the princes to "kill the mad dogs."[23] Not unlike Augustine, Luther proclaimed a "two kingdom" doctrine, which affirmed princes as legitimate rulers best equipped "to patch and darn as best we can while we live, punish abuses and lay bandages and poultices over the sores" within the temporal realm.

Critics of Erasmus accused him of having "laid the egg" hatched by Luther. Erasmus responded saying Luther had "hatched a different bird entirely."[24] Erasmus's concerns aside, history recognizes Luther as initiator of the Protestant Reformation. Popular tradition indicates that he nailed his Ninety-Five Theses to the door of the church in Wittenberg on All Saints' Day (31 October) in 1517, calling for a public debate on indulgences and related matters, which led to his excommunication by Pope Leo X in 1521.

Huldrych Zwingli (1484–1531) was at the forefront of political confrontation with political leaders in Zurich. Luther initially described him as the "Giant of Zurich" but later accused him of lapsing into superstition concerning the real presence of Christ in the bread and wine of the Sacrament of Holy Communion. The theology and political ethics of John Calvin (1509–1564) were, in turn, born in confrontation with the authorities in the city of Geneva, from which he was initially expelled by the city fathers, before later being entreated to return after the city was plunged into lawlessness. While Luther enjoyed the friendship and support of Frederick III, elector of Saxony, Calvin lived in conflict with Geneva city leaders, demanding that they obey the commandments of God as decreed by (Calvin's) Geneva church council.

Luther's response to the princes as opposed to Zwingli's and Calvin's responses to civil authority imposed a lasting divide in Protestantism. Critics of Luther's cooperation with the princes through a two-kingdom

---

and Greek Church."

23. Porter, ed., *Luther: His Political Writings*.

24. Reynolds, "Was Erasmus Responsible for Luther?"

doctrine have over the years accused Lutherans of being too close to secular authority. Zwingli and Calvin (viewed as the fathers of the Reformed tradition) conversely came to be seen by their detractors as opening the door to theocratic rule. In Germany many Lutherans allied themselves with secular authorities. For example, noted Lutheran intellectuals and clergy endorsed Kaiser Wilhelm's policies in 1914 and supported the German Christian movement during the Third Reich in the 1930s. The excesses of Calvinism are seen in the influence of neo-Calvinists on theologized brands of politics that degenerated into theological support for apartheid politics in South Africa (condemned as heresy by the World Alliance of Reformed Churches in 1982), Protestant extremism in Northern Ireland, and other narrow brands of nationalism.

Radical Protestant Reformation

Anabaptists, Spiritualists, Pietists, and Evangelical Rationalists in Europe and the Puritan Reformers in England are commonly regarded as radical reformers. In their commitment to the purification of the church, they opposed cooperation with the state as forms of Augustinian and Lutheran excess.

Prominent among radical reformers committed to political activism were Thomas Müntzer, Andreas Karlstadt, the Zwickau prophets in Germany, and Konrad Grebel and Felix Mantz in Zurich. Spiritualists and Pietists in Protestant churches were committed to many of the same theological principles as other radical reformers while being principally committed to nonviolence. These groups included Mennonites, Hutterites, Unitarians, Brethren, and other so-called restorationist churches.

The Catholic Reformation

In the meantime, opposition to ecclesial corruption, including to the appointment of absentee bishops, to the sale of indulgences, to earlier papal crusades, and to the church's support for the invasion of the Americas, was escalating within the Catholic Church.

John Wycliffe, a philosopher, theologian, and biblical scholar in Oxford and Jan Hus, a Bohemian priest, were condemned as heretics for their involvement in the struggle for renewal in the fourteenth and fifteenth centuries. Dominican, Benedictine, Trappist, and Franciscan communities and the Society of Jesus (Jesuits) were at the forefront of Catholic reform that led to the convening of the Council of Trent (1545–1563), which took the institutional lead in the Catholic Reformation.

Puritanism

Influenced by the reformations in Europe, significant groups of Protestant antagonists took refuge in parts of Britain, divided between nonseparating Puritans committed to reform within the Church of England and separatists, who broke away from the established church. The separatists in particular found common cause with parliamentary opposition to Royalists at the beginning of the English Civil War (1642–1646). Oliver Cromwell, a self-styled "Puritan Moses," supported the death of Charles I, became Lord Protector of the Commonwealth of England, and headed the Cromwellian Republic (1649–1658). Following the restoration of the monarchy in 1660 some separatists adopted a moderate response to the crown, supporting the coronation of Charles II as king of England, while others rallied under the slogan of "no Bishop, no King." Nonconformism grew in Wales. In Scotland, John Knox used the discontent of Protestants to promote a form of religious nationalism that resulted in the removal of Mary Queen of Scots from the throne and in Northern Ireland separating from the south of Ireland.

American Puritanism

Formative to the spread of Puritanism was the Great Migration between 1630 and 1640, when over twenty thousand settlers migrated to the "New World" largely in response to the restraints on religious reform in England. John Winthrop, a leading figure in the founding of the Massachusetts Bay Colony, envisaged a "City upon a Hill" and a Commonwealth in continuity with separatist values, free from the dictates of the English crown and the Church of England. Other separatists established colonies in Connecticut and elsewhere. Nonseparatists affirmed their loyalty to the Church of England. Yet other settlers started holiness movements inspired by the teaching of George Whitefield, and John and Charles Wesley; these movements in turn led to the establishment of the Methodist Episcopal Church in 1784, which later united with other Methodist breakaway groups from the Church of England. Other settlers rejoined or affirmed their loyalty to the Church of England: for instance, the Episcopal Church in America was founded in 1789.

Political developments, theological disputes, and internal conflicts intensified in New England. Relations with native tribes deteriorated, largely as result of settler-borne diseases and land disputes. Puritan groups began to leave New England, extending their theological and social visions across the country. This migration included Presbyterians and other Protestant churches. Some churches demanded the right to determine church polity, confessions and practices at a local or congregational level, rather than at a regional or national level. These churches eventually united with other autonomous congregations, leading to the establishment of Congregational and Baptist Churches.[25] Collectively, they contributed to a brand of American Protestantism that today includes conservative evangelicals, Pentecostals, the Apostolic Faith Mission, Full Gospel churches, and the Southern Baptist Convention—all of which influence Christianity in America and through their evangelical mission work across the world.

Alexis de Tocqueville argued that despite the "harshness and bigotry of the early colonists" and their beliefs, Puritanism in America gave rise to a spirit of competitiveness that shaped American entrepreneurship and independence, and that continues to be part of the American milieu.[26]

The Escalation of Nationalism

The past two thousand years have seen the persecution of the early church, the rapprochement of church and state through the Edict of Milan, plus mutual manipulation of emperors and kings on the one hand and popes and bishops on the other. Throughout this history, the struggle for Christian integrity, inspired by a resistant minority within the church, has both challenged and disrupted the coexistence of state and church.

The dominant response of the Christian church has been to reach some level of coexistence with different states. There have, throughout history, simultaneously been individuals and collectives in the Christian tradition who have resisted the compromises of church institutions by upholding the prophetic traditions of resistance and liberation within Christian history. This was notable in the Confessing Church in Nazi Germany, is evident in the history of martyrs throughout the world and underpins

25. See Knight, *Orthodoxies in Massachusetts*.
26. Tocqueville, *Democracy in America*, chapter 5.

the liberation theologies in Latin America, Black theology in the United States, feminist theology, and the Kairos movements in apartheid South Africa and Palestine.

Important for the purposes of this study is whether there is a particular ingredient to religion that erroneously lends itself, consciously or otherwise, to seeing divinity symbolized in a head of state (a monarch, national leader, or caliph). This partly explains why the divide between traditional Augustinian and alternative church-state doctrines continues to be pertinent to the involvement of the church in community and national politics.

Religious Extremism

Richard Rohr provides a telling critique of Christianity's preoccupation with doctrinal detail, negotiated under the authority of the Roman emperor in 325 CE, to which Rohr attributes the emasculation of the spiritual and ethical dimensions of Jesus' ministry that appear in the Gospels. "Ask someone whether he or she is a believer," he suggests, and the chances are the response will be in "doctrinal language," contributing to "an antiquarian society that prefers to look backward instead of forward."[27] Rohr argues that the contemporary church is its own theological enemy, tethered as it is to philosophical abstraction instead of to "the real, historical, flesh-and-blood Jesus of Nazareth."[28] Jesus, Rohr reminds us, sent his apostles into the world to heal the brokenhearted, care for the widow and orphan, and love both neighbors and strangers—not to create "doctrinally correct" believers. This abstraction captures what Carl Michalson identified as the "empty history" of liberal Christianity in the West.

27. See Rohr's meditations between January 8 and January 24, 2019, in his online meditation archive. On doctrinal language, see Rohr, "Belief or Discipleship?" On an antiquarian, backward-looking society, see Rohr, "Many Ways of Knowing." For the phrase "the real, flesh-and-blood Jesus of Nazareth," see Rohr, "Practical Christianity."

28. Rohr, "Practical Christianity."

5

Islam: Allah—Far and Near

ISLAM IS THE WORLD's largest religion after Christianity and, according to the Pew Research Center, is likely to be the largest by 2070. It is at the same time the least understood and most maligned of the Abrahamic faiths in the West, with jingoistic and mass-media responses to the 9/11 tragedy exacerbating this animosity. The stigmatization of Islam in the West, typified in the Crusades and the expulsion of Muslims from Spain, reached new levels with European colonization in the wake of Napoleon's invasion of Egypt in 1798. This spawned a spread of facile and static perceptions of Islam and of European superiority in orientalist literature in the West.[1]

Arguably the deepest form of religious truth is known only to those who are the true and most devout practitioners of their particular religion. There is, however, no single voice in any religion, only a bundle of continuities and discontinuities. Kwame Anthony Appiah suggests that only "fundamentalists [literalists] and militant atheists make the dubious assumption that religion entails a fixed set of scripturally determined beliefs."[2] What follows is written primarily for and from within a Western perspective which views Islam as essentially "other" and "different." The intent here is to by-pass disparaging populism among Jewish and Christian fundamentalists and Western-based ideologues on Islam.[3]

1. Said, *Orientalism*.

2. Appiah, *Lies That Bind*.

3. Raised and educated in a liberal Christian tradition I have over the years become increasingly absorbed by the often neglected beliefs in the ineffability of ultimate truth upheld in the Abrahamic faiths and, not least, in the incomparability of divine transcendence. I suggest that neither science nor religion provides an adequate answer to the

Islam, like all religions, has been influenced by global and regional power relations, including tribal conflicts, the experience of Western colonialism, and disputes resulting from military conquest, trade, and expansion beyond the Arabian Peninsula into Iberia and the West, the Indian subcontinent and Afghanistan. In order to understand each of these developments, one must put forth a concerted effort to grasp the religious nuances involved, not to mention the perspectives of other religions. James Baldwin, the American civil rights activist and author, captures the difficulty involved in understanding identity difference: "History is not merely something to be read. And it does not refer merely, or even principally, to the past. On the contrary, the great force of history comes from the fact that we carry it within us, are unconsciously controlled by it in many ways, and history is literally present in all that we do. It could scarcely be otherwise, since it is to history that we owe our frames of reference, our identities, and our aspirations."[4]

Noteworthy in this regard is that scientific thought is an inherent part of the Islamic Golden Age, extending from the eighth century to the thirteenth century, during which astronomy, mathematics, medicine, and related subjects were drawn into theological debate. Although the Golden Age is commonly regarded as terminating with the Mongol invasions and the siege of Baghdad in 1258 CE, the influence of science survived through later centuries. Without exception, the influence of science on Islamic theology declined as a result of growing alliances between doctrinaire Islam and political power. The impact of social sciences and difficulties confronting modern Islamic states, as well as internal and regional political and military conflict, has ensured that scientific worldviews will be challenged in Muslim countries. That is to say, Islam is not alone, but, like Judaism, Christianity, and other world religions, will likely face challenges from alternative worldviews.

---

ultimate mysteries of life. Recognizing the limitations of comparative religion and interfaith dialogue, both of which are often "too polite" to pursue this conundrum, I suggest that a cross-disciplined, transversal debate between science and the nuances of different religions offers an opportunity to explore again the reality of the "great unknown." I am particularly mindful that believers and linguists find a depth of meaning in Arabic and other Semitic languages to which I only have indirect access. Guided by Arabic-speaking colleagues I have used parallel Arabic-English presentations of the Qur'an, taking full responsibility for a nominal and appreciative quest for a deeper understanding of Islam. To borrow Tony Judt's phrase, what follows is written "in good faith."

4. This quotation is from Baldwin, "Unnameable Objects, Unspeakable Crimes."

The Five Pillars of Islam, *Shahadah*, continue, however, to be the primary theological and ethical lens through which it seeks to engage the world. This is captured in Confession of Faith ("there is no god but Allah, and Muhammad is the messenger of Allah"); in *Salat*, prayer; in *Zakat*, almsgiving; in *Sawm*, fasting; and in *Haj*, pilgrimage. These pillars capture the absolute transcendence and the presence of Allah "far and near," in the "east and west . . . wherever you may turn" (Qur'an 2:115); the prayer and deeper meaning of the sacred text that requires us to listen to the word (advice) and the best results thereof (Qur'an 39:18); communal belonging and almsgiving, (Qur'an 2:103–4); fasting and the sacred ritual pilgrimage to Mecca (Qur'an 2:196). The first basic Islamic code of conduct was established under the leadership of the Prophet Muhammad at Medina in 622 CE. Yet, as in the other Abrahamic religions, institutional Islam led to internal divisions—not least between Sunni and Shi'ite Muslims. This led in the ninth and tenth centuries to the four main Sunni schools of law, namely, the Hanafi, Maliki, Shafi'i, and Hanbali *madhhabs*. Shi'ite (or Shia) schools, in turn, include those of the Twelvers, Ja'fari, and Zaidiyyah. As recently as 2005 two hundred prominent Islamic jurists, recognized by eight legitimate Sunni and Shi'ite schools of law, protested chiefly against Muslim-majority countries that violated clerical law as understood in the Qur'an and Hadith.[5]

From the perspective of the fast-moving world of religious and cultural disputes in the West, Islam shows a level of consistency typified in the absolute, unique transcendence of God (Allah). The essence of this belief can scarcely be theologically questioned or rejected by any open-minded Jewish or Christian believer.[6] Other differences aside, the transcendence of God is the basis of Jewish-Christian-Islamic metaphysical harmony. The Prophet Muhammad is the Seal of the Prophets but not divine, and the Qur'an is the pure word of God but not God. The praxis of Islam is expressed through a common identity that includes prayer, almsgiving, and pilgrimage, which symbolizes a commitment to rise above all national, political, and related identities and distractions. As products of different historical journeys and characterized by diverse identities and the evolution of

5. I have used the standard (English) translation from Arabic in what follows. The word *Shi'ite* is a Latinized form for the Arabic *Shi'i*, with the plural *Shi'ites*, while in recent literature *Shia* has been used to refer to the collective group, which is a direct transliteration of the Arabic word. Popular writings have, in turn, come to omit the apostrophe (which stands for a guttural consonant).

6. See Sacks, *Great Partnership*, 252.

cultures and practices, Judaism, Christianity, and Islam have failed to live up to their highest ideals and beliefs.

The Transcendence of Allah

"To Allah belongs the East and the West, whithersoever you turn, there is Allah's countenance, incomparable, surpassing all human description and knowledge" (Qur'an 2:115). Allah is transcendent and close to the believer, both far and near. In continuity with the response to Moses's question concerning the person of God in the book of Exodus, "I am who I am" (Exod 3:14), the ineffable transcendence of Allah is the decisive first principle of Islam.

The doctrine of *tawhid* (the oneness of God) extends beyond the notion of a monotheistic God. It comprises a sense of total oneness and unity that embraces all of life. In the classical sense, God is Being rather than a being, and the ground of all creation. Allah is Wholly Other, beyond comprehension, imagination, or definition, while being seen in all that exists: "He is Allah, the Creator, the Originator, the Fashioner, to Him belong the most beautiful names: whatever is in the heaven and on earth" (Qur'an 59:24). He is seen in whatever is beautiful and terrible in nature and humanity. Allah is both "far" and "near." "In the midst of His nearness He is far, and in the midst of His similarity He is incomparable."[7]

Institutional Islam has often deviated from its own belief in the transcendent incomparability of Allah, capitulating to racist, ethnic, gendered, tribal, and nationalist tendencies, as well as to overt and insidious forms of theocracy. No religion or ideology in history has consistently avoided similar egocentricity. It is seen in militant Zionism, in the entrenched neo-conservative Christianity of Western foreign policy, and in the jihadist ideology of the Islamic State. History holds ample evidence that anger, greed, and the will to power are controlling passions that know no partiality to any creed or religion. Desperation and extremism breed counterdesperation and counterextremism.

In dividing the world into good and evil, religious extremism exacts a heavy toll on humankind, in both concealed and overt ways. Violent jihadists regard religious discipline (jihad) as the pursuit of a pending global and cosmic war that will destroy Western domination and purify Islam. Originating in the seventh century, jihad emerged as a reaction against polytheistic gods

7. Murata and Chittick, *Vision of Islam*, 72–73.

and a "time of ignorance" or disbelief. Extremists deem their war to be a mirror of a metaphysical war in the transcendent realm that will usher in the ultimate victory of God over Satan and an age of eternal peace on earth. The magnitude of such perceived godly or holy war means there can be no compromise or surrender. It is a fight to the end.[8]

The warning is clear. Inasmuch as responsible theology affirms the dialectic between the distance and the proximity of divine revelation, it has an obligation to counter extremism. For inherent in this obligation is a recognition of the limits of human knowledge and deliberation vis-à-vis the ineffability of divine or ultimate truth within each changing scene of life. This makes for a theological imperative of vigilance and self-critique, of resisting the temptation to read a contemporary crisis through the literalistic lens of an archetypical or iconic text in the Bible or Qur'an. It involves rather the complex task of seeking to uncover the context of historical events *as well as* the scripted and linguistic reporting of these events in foundational texts and traditions.

As I suggested in the earlier chapters on Judaism and Christianity, there is no direct, literalistic step from sacred text to contemporary experience in formal Islam to support the values of extremists. The presence of the complexities of each new age invariably enables the rich and powerful to use religion to serve their own needs. The risks of extremism in the name of God plague Judeo-Christian-Islamic relations in contemporary politics. It has been epitomized in Western colonization of the Arabian Peninsula, the Levant, and the Maghreb, as well as of North America, Asia, and Africa. It has involved statesmen, aspiring empire builders, and religious propagandists. Christian missionaries, explorers, adventurers, and traders, in turn, ventured into what they declared as terra nullius—literally, empty land—which could therefore be legally seized to advance Christian colonialism, in a venture Rudyard Kipling vividly memorialized as the "White Man's Burden."[9]

These developments inspired scholars, opinion makers, and the media to create swathes of literature that constructed stereotypes of the Middle East, penetratingly described in Edward Said's *Orientalism*. These stereotypes contributed to popular negative perceptions of Islam in the West

8. Aslan, *Beyond Fundamentalism*.

9. Kipling, "White Man's Burden." Kipling's poem specifically was an exhortation to the United States to colonize the Philippines, but the phrase is often used to describe the—arrogant—logic of colonialism.

that led to the 1916 Sykes-Picot Agreement and later the occupation of the Middle East in the wake of World War I. In the aftermath of the Allied victory, the French intensified their presence in Algeria, Morocco, Tunisia, Mauritania, and much of the Western Sahara, while Britain extended and consolidated its authority in Yemen, Iraq, Palestine, Jordan, Egypt, and Sudan as well as in much of sub-Saharan Africa.

The granting of the Palestine Mandate by the League of Nations to Britain saw the growth of Jewish and Christian support for Zionism. This further alienated Muslims in the former Ottoman Empire, reenergizing Islamic nationalism and intensifying religious sensitivities among grassroots believers, who rallied behind the call of political and religious ideologues. The marginalization of Islamic culture by the Western occupation forces led to an intensified backlash by the majority of citizens, and when colonial powers withdrew from occupied territories in the mid-twentieth century, postcolonial proposals on secular rule, underpinned by Western democracy, found limited support among Muslims. Most traditional and moderate believers rejected these proposals as forms of neocolonialism, while extremist jihadists resisted both traditionalists and moderates for deviating from a literalist understanding of the pure and infallible meaning of the Qur'an.

Uncompromising and escalating partisanship in and between Muslim states has led to the undermining of the traditional Islamic affirmation that God (Allah) is absolutely transcendent, ineffable, and omniscient. The resultant division between radical, moderate, and traditional Muslims has, at the same time, come to be seen by progressive Islamic scholars as an abiding reminder of the need for a corrective to populist and institutional surrender to transient egotistical, racist, tribal, and nationalist events in history.

The Qur'an

The Qur'an is regarded by Muslims as the pure Word of Allah delivered to Muhammad. Formal reading or recitation of the Qur'an requires, according to Islamic custom and tradition, prescribed rituals and phonic awareness. Reciters are instructed to "recite the Qur'an with rhythmic chant" (73:4) to ensure it makes "skins tremble" and "hearts soften" (39:23) when it is heard by the faithful. "Those who listen to the Word and follow the best meaning in it are the ones whom God has guided, and the ones imbued with understanding" (39:18).

Not fully understood in the West, the Qur'an is sometimes dismissed as an incoherent, apocalyptic text created by Muhammad, a shrewd political strategist. Even Huston Smith, known for his deep respect for Islam and other world religions, argues that "no one has ever curled up on a rainy weekend to read the Qur'an." A pious imam replied: "That is because Allah's word is better understood with due respect, through the appropriate ritual, phonics and posture."

The authority of the Qur'an in populist Islam is similar to the traditional submission of orthodox Judaism to the Torah and the response of Christian fundamentalists to the Bible. The challenge within these traditions concerns the interpretation of a text, and throughout history it has resulted in divisions between absolutist and unequivocal literalists on the one hand and those who seek to understand the essence or spiritual intent of the text on the other. Nonliteralist traditional believers, traditional moderates, and reformers scrutinize the philology, context, and history of interpretation of a text within a given tradition. Unlike most mainline Christians, who see literalism negatively, most Muslims, including moderates and reformers, regard themselves essentially as fundamentalists, who seek to understand the depths or fundamental meaning of the Qur'anic text.

Viewed as the culmination of all previous revelations in the Hebrew and Christian scripture, the Qur'an, like the Bible, includes parables, similitudes, allegories, stories, and contradictions that, taken in context, convey community prejudices as well as important insights, spiritual teachings, warnings, and admonitions for the faithful. Reformers and rationalists suggest this requires interpretative caution and restraint in understanding the global meaning of God's revelation in the Qur'an as well as in the Hadith, the sacred words of Allah *(hadith qudsi)* or the noble utterances of Muhammad *(hadith sharif)* (Qur'an 39:27). Just as Jews and Christians have offered multiple interpretations of their foundational texts given the circumstances in which they have found themselves, so Muslims have had different understandings of what constitutes righteous living in relation to the changing demands of existence. For literalists, the Qur'an, delivered to Muhammad in seventh-century Arabia, was the *uncreated, timeless* word of Allah, devoid of the influence of the broader historical or social context at the time. Moderates and reformers, while affirming the eternal validity of the Qur'an as the word of God, argue that the only reasonable method of exegesis (not least in a situation of rapidly changing consciousness) is to recognize the distance between the historical context within which the text was delivered to Muhammad and the historical context within which the text is now being read, understood, and interpreted.[10] Qur'anic interpretation is undertaken as a sacred duty (Qur'an 16:92), in order to affirm the *Shahadah* ("There is no God but God, and Muhammad is his messenger.") and to execute the Five Pillars of Islam. So the theological distance between literalists and traditional moderates may well be an example—and an escalation—of a strain evident across Islamic history and continuing today, discernible as it is in contemporary scholarship.

Abdulkader Tayob traces this debate between theological literalists and moderates back to the time of the death of the Prophet and to the spread of Islam across cultures, languages, and dialects.[11] In his 2019 University of Cape Town summer school lectures, Tayob provides an overview of Islamic philosophy, beginning with the writing of Shafi'i (767–820 CE), who developed a set of guidelines for interpreting the Qur'an and Hadith. To this Tayob adds the voices of other formative exegetes: Mawardi (974–1058 CE), who turned to philosophers, poets, and Sufis to portray the depths of the Qur'an; Ghazali (1058–1111 CE), who wrote on the inevitability of doubt when reading the text through the lens of reason, but who affirmed the importance of worship, charity, and pilgrimage; and Ibn Rushd, known in English as Averroes (1126–1198 CE)—all of these sought to bridge the gap between the intelligentsia and grassroots believers by focusing on allegorical similarities between philosophical and scientific truths and the Qur'an. The spirituality of Rumi (1207–1273 CE) took the debate to a broader, universal level, portraying the presence of the divine in the depths of all creation and all religions: "Praying and fasting as a Muslim, he challenged the hypocritical and one-dimensional 'religion' that is always the enemy of real spirituality."[12] In resistance to a negative Western perspective on civilization in the wake of twentieth-century world wars, Fazlur Rahman (1919–1988) and others revived the reintegration of the

---

10. See, inter alia: Abou El Fadl, *Great Theft*; Aslan, *No God but God*.

11. I am indebted to Abdulkader Tayob, Professor of Islamic Studies at the University of Cape Town, who on several occasions discussed with me the history of Islamic philosophy, giving me consent to draw on his (presently) unpublished manuscript, based on his January 2019 Summer School lectures, *A Journey through Critical and Philosophical Reconstructions of Islam*. I acknowledge his guidance and the access to his written text with gratitude, while taking full responsibility for any misunderstanding of his insights in the pages that follow.

12. Helminski, "Introduction."

Qur'an, Hadith, and philosophy with a view to articulating the founding principles inherent to the earlier history of Islam.

Contemporary analyst of faith and culture Nahed Artoul Zehr portrays the depth of Islamic hermeneutical plurality through four categories: "literalists," "traditionalists," "modernists," and "secularists."[13] Referring to the different interpretations of Islam in his work *The Great Theft: Wrestling Islam from the Extremists*, Islamic law scholar Abou El Fadl (reflecting a measure of frustration with literalists) argues that "many Muslims are woefully ignorant about their own religion" and contends that literalism contradicts the "Muslim psyche, the foundational message of the Qur'an, the quintessential lessons taught by the Muhammad, the moral priorities of the individual believer and ethical parameters that guide Muslims in interaction with others."[14] He supports a faith that upholds the essential principles of Islam, which he argues can be reconciled with the challenges of modernity. This, he suggests, coincides with the belief of the "silent majority of Muslims." He thus opens the door optimistically to what he suggests could become "a transformative moment" no less dramatic than the Reformation that swept through Europe in the sixteenth century.[15]

Questioning literalism gained momentum in the Abbasid Empire, which succeeded the Umayyads in 750 CE and specifically through the tutelage of Ibn Rushd. The scholarship of Ibn Rushd, seen by many Muslims as veering (too far) in favor of Aristotelian philosophy and rationalism, is queried by "critical traditionalists," among them Ebrahim Moosa. Drawing on Abu Hamid al-Ghazali, Moosa observes a need to straddle the liminal space between rationalism and traditional Islam, which holds the "creativity of the human spirit" as it seeks "solutions to humanity's [recurring] existential crises."[16] As I suggested in Chapter 2, the provocation of Ibn Rushd nevertheless continues to be a source of inspiration that underpins moderate and progressive theology in contemporary Islam.

The continuum between the vulnerability of *traditional believers* as they contemplate the extent and pace of change in the modern world is discussed by Ebrahim Rasool. Analyzing the prevailing milieu in Islam, he characterizes extremists as a minority of alienated believers who are seeking psychological security through unqualified belief in the Qur'an as

13. Zehr, *War against al-Qaeda*.

14. Abou El Fadl, *Great Theft*, 6–11; see also Zehr, *War against al-Qaeda*.

15. Abou El Fadl, *Great Theft*, 5–6.

16. Moosa, *Ghazali and the Poetics of Imagination*, 2–29, 261–62.

the literal word of God. Eager to share their newly discovered assurance of God's blessing, they grow in confidence amid a minority of supportive extremists. They are often funded by nefarious religious splinter groups and as their funds grow, their confidence grows. Trapped in the unfolding drama of psychological spiritual perplexity, a growing minority of believers feel compelled to do something about the prevailing situation of exploitation, greed, and domination they experience. This makes them vulnerable to recruitment into terror groups that offer a sense of belonging in a purposeful community along with the promise of a source of income and a fear of revenge if they decline recruitment. Like any "good soldier" in a dirty war, they are persuaded to pay the ultimate price for their beliefs, and violence becomes an end in itself.[17] Reza Aslan cites a document discovered in the luggage of the 9/11 hijackers: "Pray the supplication as you leave your hotel . . . Before you step aboard the plane, pray the supplication. At the moments of death, pray . . . Remember, this is a battle for the sake of God. The enemies are the allies of Satan . . . And when the hour approaches, welcome death for the sake of God. With your last breath remember God. Make your final words 'There is no god but God.'"[18]

As I suggested earlier, there is a deep vulnerability in dogmatic monotheism that tempts zealous believers and ideologues to reduce the ineffability of a transcendent and universal God to the finite constructs of a particular nation, religion, gender, or culture. The firm belief in the Abrahamic faiths is that every person is created in the image of God, yet history abounds with perceptions that those who do not share the beliefs of a particular community are outside the realm of God's protection or care. This assertion explains Islamic declarations of apostasy and heresy against other Muslims, which have led to abuse and even death. Widespread death clearly occurred in the Crusades, other holy wars and genocides. It is at the root of hostility between Sunni and Shi'ite Muslims, in Zionist extremism, and in the violence of White supremacists and the Christian Right.

The *salaam* verses in the Qur'an, the Hebrew Bible, and New Testament are clear, and are there to be celebrated. However, the failure of religious institutions to acknowledge and repudiate atrocities, as advocated in foundational texts, leaves many thoughtful people increasingly skeptical of religious moralism within the context of diverse religious, cultural, gender-sensitive communities.

17. Rasool, Unpublished manuscript (2016), chapter 4.
18. Quoted in Aslan, *Beyond Fundamentalism*, 3.

Each faith at the same time recognizes that in crises, the prophets and messiahs of Judaism and Christianity (recognized in the Qur'an), as well as Muhammad, his companions, intellectuals, and martyrs in Islam, call their wayward followers back to obedience. Responding to current forms of violence in Islamic communities, many believers are reclaiming this corrective tradition in Islam, insisting, "we can no longer afford to refuse to critically engage our tradition."[19]

Identity

The essence of Islamic identity in the West is otherness and difference, embedded in the history of transmission of tradition traced back to the Prophet and his companions, the emergence of Islamic civilization and custom, jurisprudence, and theological interpretation. This identity is traditionally expressed in Islamic culture through dress, ornamentation, architecture, calligraphy, music, ritual, social custom, and cuisine. Beautiful and exotic, it is often caricatured by adversaries as a mask for evil and can provoke violent confrontation, as seen in the Charlie Hebdo cartoons in 2015.[20] Armando Salvatore problematizes the nature of Islamic identity, arguing that despite European and secular components practiced among some Muslims, there is a "non-European" dimension to contemporary Muslim culture, overlooked by Western scholars who reduce this reality to a deep-seated reluctance in Islam to adapt to modernization, as defined in the West.[21]

Like traditional Judaism, Islam has a particular communal presence and self-awareness. It is less prominent than in Christianity, which affirms a universal sense of identity as expressed in the teachings of Saint Paul: "neither Jew nor Greek . . . for you are all one in Christ" (Gal 3: 28). This Christian inclusivity very quickly lapsed into political expediency, however, most markedly with the Edict of Milan in 313 CE, which gave rise to a problematic synthesis between church and empire that continues to be the hallmark of Christianity in the West. The Qur'an explains the unity and difference between tribes and subtribes in a more nuanced way, arguing that diversity needs to be recognized and respected as part of the unity of faith: prioritizing the need to "know each other" (Qur'an 49: 13) without ceasing to be diverse. Despite emphasizing the need for hospitality and inclusivity, this goal

19. See Abou El Fadl, *Great Theft*; Na'im, *Islam and Human Rights*.

20. Rasool, "Charlie Hebdo."

21. See Salvatore, *Sociology of Islam*.

remains aspirational and is often undermined by historical hostility between Muslims in the Middle East, Southeast Asia, and elsewhere.

The flip side of this isolation is the insidious group-think intrigue that is so often a product of separation. The danger of all in-groups is that "knowing," whether within and without one's own tribe or religion, can lapse into a failure to heed the otherness and transcendence of Allah, who, the Qur'an teaches, is the impartial judge of all individuals and groups on the basis of inward intent and behavior rather than words and ritual. This ethical awareness leaves Islam critical of the secular empty or naked state, which it sees as generating atomistic individualism and alliances of collective interest that neglect the ethical imperative of Islam and the religions of the Book.[22] Recognizing that Jews and Christians have heard God's word through their own messengers, political culture has often lapsed into using subtle and not-so-subtle religious metaphors negatively to fuel interreligious conflict. This is seen in the culture of the United States and the West, no less than in Muslim hegemonic extremism in the Middle East, Pakistan, and Afghanistan. This was seen in the 1979 Iranian Revolution, the emergence of the Taliban, and more recently in the Islamic State and similar organizations.

A retrospective on these events suggests the need for critical self-examination of religious revolutionary idealism in Islam no less than in other religions, as a basis for coexistence between religions and for mutual respect in an escalating global conflict. A careful reading of the Qur'an through the lenses of moderate Islam rejects what traditionalist literalists regard as the need to assert Muslim priority over other religions. The equivalent of Jewish and Christian religious bigotry is seen in the Islamic practice of *takfir*, which defines opponents of diverse groups within Islam and in other religions as infidels and worthy of condemnation. Extremist Wahhabis, not to mention other extremist groups, have been commonly seen as the most potent form of Islamic extremism on the planet. Yet their selective and literalistic use of the Qur'an represents a violation of the all-encompassing message of the Prophet Muhammad.

A moderate reading of community is a very different one. It is part of a section of the Qur'an called "The Feast" (Qur'an 5:43–48). This involves coexistence, kindness, justice, and cooperation with the People of the Book, described as "Christians, Jews and Sabians" (Qur'an 5:69; 2:62), in response to the Qur'anic belief that there are different paths to salvation,

22. See Lawrence, *Defenders of God*; see also Juergensmeyer, *Global Rebellion*.

and that all humanity will be judged on the basis of righteous living on the day of the final judgment.

Back to the Beginning

Any suggestion of a single, monolithic Islamic theology is both inaccurate and misleading. Negative perceptions are often not the fault of Islam per se, but of a human propensity to appropriate whatever religious and other ideas are available in order to further greed, ambition, and power.

The Prophet Muhammad and Companions

Muhammad (570–632 CE) was born into an exploitative religioeconomic situation in Mecca, where polytheists, Zoroastrians, Arab Jews, and Christians shared in the economic gains associated with the Ka'ba shrine, under the control of the Quraysh tribe to which his extended family belonged. Raised in the desert by a foster mother in accordance with ancient Arab custom, Muhammad was later cared for by his grandfather and subsequently employed by his uncle Abu Talib, a wealthy merchant. He married the widowed Kadija bint Khuwaylid, a businesswoman, who would become known as the mother of Islam.

Troubled by his privileged position relative to the deprivations of the poor, Muhammad withdrew at age forty into the desert for contemplation and reflection. As he was engaged in meditation in the Cave of Hira on Mount Jabal an-Nur, he was overwhelmed by the invisible presence of the Archangel Gabriel who, over a twenty-three-year period, delivered to him what traditional Muslims believe is the unchanging, infallible, and inerrant word of God.

The deaths of Muhammad's uncle and his wife in the same year (620 CE) left him politically isolated, financially vulnerable, and emotionally devastated. Fearing for his life, he fled to Medina together with a Meccan elder and close friend, Abu Bakr—an event commemorated as the *Hijrah* (migration). In Medina, Muhammad emerged as a community leader, eventually organizing raids on enemy tribes and initiating what would become a Muslim confederacy of tribes or states. The conflicts led to the eventual occupation of Mecca by Muhammad and his allies, during which he undercut the religious ideology and economic practices associated with the Ka'ba, cleansing it of idols and murals that had been dedicated to the invisible Allah.

By the time of Muhammad's death in 632 CE, he was regarded as the "Seal of the Prophets"—the culmination of all prophets, including Moses and Jesus, sent by Allah. Responding to Muhammad as the final prophet, subsequent generations of intellectuals, mystics, rulers, and theologians continue to debate the hermeneutics and linguistics of the Qur'an and Hadith in their attempts to understand the depths of historic revelation of Allah to Muhammad.

The Prophet's companions are reported to have elected Abu Bakr, the father-in law of Muhammad, as caliph. He was followed by Umar (`Umar ibn al-Khattab), Uthman (`Uthmān ibn 'Affān), and Ali ('Ali ibn Abi Talib), all of whom are regarded by Sunnis as the "rightly guided" caliphs. The Shi'ites, as the devotees of Ali became known (*shi'atu 'Ali* or followers of Ali) declared that only Ali was "rightly guided." After Umar and Uthman were murdered and Ali was assassinated in the Great Mosque of Kufa in 661 CE, Ali's son, Hasan, declined to succeed his father, apparently in an attempt to avoid growing conflict in the community. This opened the way for the strongman of the time, Muawiyah I, who, as newly elected caliph, established the dynasty of Umayyad caliphs.[23]

Sunni, Shi'ite, and Sufi

If Jews, Christians, and others know naught else about Islam, they know that Muslims are divided between Sunnis and Shi'ites. Globally, 10 to 20 percent of Muslims are Shi'ite, mostly concentrated in Iran, Iraq, Azerbaijan, and Bahrain, where Shi'ites make up a majority of the total population. There are also sizeable Shi'ite populations in Pakistan, India, Albania, Bosnia-Herzegovina, Lebanon, and parts of the Horn of Africa.[24] The Sunni comprise between 80 and 90 percent of the global Muslim population, with the remainder belonging to other Muslim communities.

Crucial to the development of this demography was the death of 'Alī ibn Abī Ṭālib, commonly referred to as Ali, the fourth caliph. Ali's second son (and grandson of Muhammad), Husayn ibn Ali, refused to recognize Muawiyah's son and successor, Yazid, or even to accept the notion of an Islamic dynasty. Unwavering Shi'ite support for Husayn turned to anger after

23. Nasr, *Shia Revival*, 36.
24. Wikipedia, "Islam by Country" (https://en.wikipedia.org/wiki/Islam_by_country/).

his death by decapitation in the Battle of Karbala in 680 CE. The Shi'ites protested Husayn's death in what would become an annual event of lamentation and self-flagellation, linked to belief in a coming of the promised *Mahdi* or redeemer, who would prepare the way for God's Judgement Day. Animosity grew between the Sunnis and the Shi'ites, who suffered different levels of persecution, including massacres during both the Umayyad dynasty (661–750 CE) and the much longer dynasty of the Abbasids (750–1517 CE). This included the Hanbali School of jurists issuing a series of fatwas against the Shi'ites.

The division between Sunni and Shi'ites has a long and complex history, involving memory, nationalisms, politics, identity, culture, and belief. Vali Nasr, in *The Shi'ite Revival*, provides an insightful analysis of the Sunni-Shi'ite divide by distinguishing between the "Old" and the "New" Middle East. The "Old" was shaped by Arab culture and belief, centered in the ancient Sunni caliphates of Baghdad, Cairo, and Damascus. The "New" Middle East includes Sunnis and Shi'ites, cutting across the divide between Arab and non-Arab, playing itself out in Iraq, Lebanon, Syria, and elsewhere.[25] These conflicts have in more recent times been given new motivation by the Iranian Revolution of 1979 that saw the defeat of the dynasty of Mohammad Reza Shah Pahlavi, who was supported by the West. This resulted in the birth of an Islamic republic under the Shi'ite Grand Ayatollah Ruhollah Khomeini and a Shi'ite regime, which the faithful saw as being in historical continuity with Ali, the first Shi'ite caliph. The most devout Shi'ites see the Grand Ayatollah, who wears a distinctive black turban, as being in continuity with the Prophet Muhammad and Ali, whom they recognize as the first rightly guided caliph.

Earlier, unable to match the military and organizational prowess of the Sunnis, Shi'ites were sustained by a spirituality that underlay the expectation of a promised *Mahdi*, which the Shi'ite Twelver Muslims identified as Muhammad ibn Hasan al-Mahdi. They believed the *Madi*, born in approximately 868 CE, was transposed into Occultation (hiddenness) in 939 CE, and will return to earth on the day of judgment.[26]

Significantly, devout Shi'ites acclaimed Ayatollah Khomeini, the founder and the supreme leader of the Islamic Republic of Iran starting in 1979, to be the celebrated "returning Imam."

25. Nasr, *Shia Revival*, 21.
26. Nasr, *Shia Revival*, 67.

Other groups within Islam have, in turn, recognized other leaders to have been endowed with Allah's grace, power, or both, to lead Islam and these recognitions have led to the establishment of different breakaway Muslim groups. Such groups include the Ahmadiyya Jama'at, which originated with the teaching of Mirza Ghulam Ahmad in Punjab in the late nineteenth century. Regarded by mainstream Muslims as a sect outside of Islam, Ahmadiyya Jama'ats are reported to be among the fastest-growing Islamic communities in recent times.[27]

Sufism is a mystic dimension of Islam expressed through specific values, rituals, and practices. Traceable back to early Islam, Sufism is mostly practiced by Sunnis. Strictly observing Islamic law, Sufis are able to work in cooperation with various schools of Islamic jurisprudence and theology. Sufism is reflected in the dialectical thought of Ibn al-Ghazli (c. 1058–1111), who, when he experienced a crisis because of epistemological skepticism, withdrew into Sufi meditation before re-emerging as a major Sunni mystic theologian and teacher. Probing Islamic philosophy, he resolved that the ultimate truth was to be found in the mystical experience embedded in Sufi practices. Ibn 'Arabi (1165–1240), a leading Sunni mystic, in turn, described the depth of meditation as spiritual "bewilderment" or "perplexity" (hayrah), through which he experienced Allah as the "Wholly Other, beyond comprehension, imagination or definition" and yet deeply personal.[28]

Sa'diyya Shaikh, a Muslim scholar whose existential, spiritual and ethical universe is based on an Islamic worldview, draws on the insights of Ibn 'Arabi, a mentor and teacher to twelfth-century Sufi women. (He brought their identity and spiritual experiences into his broader discussions on spirituality and human capacities, and resisted the patriarchal readings of Sunni Islam that dominated at the time.) Resisting any singular, monolithic understanding of spirituality, Shaikh contends that believers and communities perceive their sense of the divine through different gender, cultural and political lenses.[29] She writes in continuity with other South African contemporary Islamic theologians that include Abdulkader Tayob, Ebrahim Moosa, Ebrahim Rasool, Farid Esack and others. Often writing in different genres, they provide a deep Qur'anic hermeneutic on contemporary issues, including political resistance to apartheid, feminist and gender prejudice, as well as class-based exploitation. Esack's examination of the contribution by feminists

27. See Fanack.com (website), "Religions in the Middle East and North Africa."
28. Almond, "Honesty of the Perplexed."
29. Shaikh, Sufi Narratives of Intimacy, 10.

across the globe offers an interpretation of different feminist values embedded in theological and secular debate in the Muslim world.[30]

Islamic Extremism

The current growth in violent extremism is commonly attributed to the writings of Sayyid Qutb (1906–1966), a theorist in the Muslim Brotherhood who was convicted of assassinating Egyptian president Gamal Abdel Nasser in 1966. The early leader of the Brotherhood was Hassan al-Banna, who espoused the idea of a just Islamic society that would depend on the moral transformation of civil society both through programs of social welfare and militant protests against governments he viewed as corrupt. His ideas inspired Islamic uprisings in India, Pakistan, and the Middle East, as well as the founding in 1988 of al-Qaeda by Osama bin Laden (1957–2011), which drew religious and secular radicalism into an alliance.

Tensions were escalating between the West, the Arabian Peninsula, and the broader Islamic world. This has been chronicled in Robert Fisk's monumental overview of the political context of this period covering the Algerian Civil War in the 1990s, the Iranian Revolution in 1979, the Iran-Iraq War between 1980 and 1988, the 1991 Gulf War, and the American invasion of Iraq in 2003, which inflamed religious and political extremism on all sides of the conflict.[31]

Born into a wealthy family in Saudi Arabia, Osama bin Laden was a dissident against the Saudi-Arabian alliance with the United States, influenced by a belief among traditional Muslims not to allow non-Muslims to be involved in intra-Muslim conflicts. He joined the army of jihadist mujahideen fighting against the communist government of Afghanistan and the Soviet Union. In 1998 he authored (in collaboration with a Palestinian Sunni theologian, Abdullah Yusuf Azzam) the "Declaration of Jihad against Jews and Crusaders," which targeted the United States, Israel, and Saudi Arabia.[32] This opened the way to violent expressions of global *jihadism*: *jihad* means simply "to strive, to apply oneself, to struggle and to persevere" for identity, religious integrity, and ethical practice. When practicing jihad, war is an absolute last resort (Qur'an 22:36–40; 2:190). The manifesto marks the beginning of al-Qaeda attacks on Western-supported apostate regimes

30 See Esack, "Islam, Feminism and Empire."

31. Fisk, *Great War for Civilization.*

32. Bin Laden, "Declaration of Jihad."

in the Arab world, including Saudi Arabia, the Assad regime in Syria, and post-Saddam Iraq, and the subsequent formation of the Islamic State of Iraq and the Levant (ISIL), which formed the caliphate of the Islamic State (IS), to resist Western involvement in the Muslim world.[33] Coterminous with this response was Shi'ite jihadism that led to Sunni-Shi'ite conflicts traceable primarily to the establishment of the Umayyad dynasty in the wake of Ali's death (in 661), and which acquired a new incentive through the 1979 (Shi'ite-led) Iranian Revolution.

The tensions between al-Qaeda and IS were further intensified as a result of a trove of correspondence following the killing of Osama bin Laden in 2011.[34] These included reports indicating bin Laden's apparent indifference to the declaration of a caliphate by ISIL's Abu Bakr al-Baghdadi, which bin Laden seems to have seen as a premature development.

An IS spokesperson declared a resounding message to the global *ummah*—"Shake off the dust of humiliation and disgrace"—in reference to the abysmal failures of secular, Western-backed Middle Eastern governments.[35] By 2014, thirty-one thousand individuals had joined its armed ranks, and the organization had accrued up to two billion US dollars through its industries of oil and gas smuggling, taxation, extortion, agriculture, kidnapping for ransom, and other criminal endeavors.[36]

In brief, to achieve its territorial exploits, IS developed and disseminated an atavistic narrative that framed itself, through a distorted notion of jihadism, as the reincarnation of an idealized interpretation of the first Sunni community. Although a minority group within Islam, jihadists understood this to have a populist appeal among alienated people who could be persuaded to support the right to use violence in order to overthrow tyranny (Qur'an 22:39–40).[37]

In all religions the impact of context, power, loyalties, and interpretation in the heat of conflict should not be overlooked in the exposition of scripture. It is here that the implications of jihadist debate are most potent and of lasting impact within Islam and the wider world. Specific jihadist

---

33. Wright, *Terror Years.*

34. Byman, "Comparing Al Qaeda and ISIS"; Fantz, "Bin Laden's Letters."

35. Quoted from a 2015 address by the then-official IS spokesperson, Abu Muhammad al-Adnani al-Shami, in International Forum for Rights and Security, *ISIS,* 44.

36. Lister, *Profiling the Islamic State,* 1–4.

37. Inter alia, Zehr, *War against al-Qaeda;* Aslan, *No God but God;* Aslan, *Beyond Fundamentalism;* Abou El Fadl, *Great Theft;* and elsewhere.

wars on the Arabian Peninsula, in Southeast Asia, and in parts of Africa, plus terror attacks in Europe, Britain, the United States, and elsewhere, come to mind in this debate. Violent brands of jihadism in these contexts address a growing array of people through policy-oriented studies and learned books as well as through social media that tout both partisan and ostensibly nonpartisan analysis of the reasons for the conflict.

At the root of literalism in contemporary Sunni Islam is Salafism, a reforming, revivalist movement that developed in Egypt in the late eighteenth century as a response to Western European imperialism. Wahhabists in turn emerged as a radical activist group closely related to Salafism. Not all Salafists are Wahhabis, but all Wahhabis are Salafists.[38] El Fadl suggests that "every single Islamic group that has achieved a degree of international infamy, such as the Taliban and al-Qaeda, has been heavily influenced by Wahhabi thought."[39] Extremist Shi'ites see themselves essentially as reformists who seek to return to the faith of the fourth caliph, Imam Ali, whom they regard as the last, and only, rightly guided caliph.

The battle between Wahhabi and Shi'ite militants for the soul of jihadism can be traced back to a disputed history relating to the division between Sunni and Shi'ite forms of Islam following the death of the fourth caliph. Both Wahhabis and Shi'ites claim theological legitimacy, both pursue violence in an uncompromising way, and both are drawn into a global dispute that they attribute to Western imperialism.

Wahhabism's violent jihadism is rooted in the vast Najid desert at the center of the Arabian Peninsula and the person of Muhammad ibn 'Abd al-Wahhab (1703–1792 CE). A devout Sunni, he became critical of what he saw as deviations from the faith of Muhammad and critical of theological and ethical compromises of the Sunni faithful, which he saw as departures from strict monotheism. These included mysticism, rationalist questioning of Muslim doctrine, and other deviations from Bedouin culture, which he saw as the embodiment of true Islam. Returning to Arabia from the Islamic diaspora, he initiated a crusade to purify Islam. Insisting on theological and ideological uniformity, he condemned the Shi'ites, dismissed Sufism as a Persian import and the intercession of the saints and the veneration of gravesites as Turkish innovations.[40] Extending his aggression against the

38. Keyscore, "Sunni Wahhabism vs. Shi'a Islam." See also Moussalli, "Wahhabism, Salafism and Islamism."

39. Abou El Fadl, *Great Theft*, 45.

40. See Aslan, *Beyond Fundamentalism*.

Ottoman Turks, whom he accused of leading Islam astray, he demanded a literal interpretation of the Qur'an.[41]

His rudimentary, decisive, and militant understanding of Islam attracted desert followers who stripped mosques of all embellishments or memorials, "cleansing" the holy cities of Mecca and Medina, destroying the tombs of the Prophet and his companions, and raiding the treasures of the Prophet's Mosque. Wahhab's followers forced men to grow beards and women to wear veils and imposed strict dietary practices. Wahhabis massacred thousands of Shi'ites on Ashura Day and smashed shrines dedicated to Ali, Husayn, and other imams.

Wahhab established an alliance with the House of Saud amid growing opposition to the encroachments of the Ottoman dynasty into Arabia. This alliance effectively made Wahhabism the primary expression of Islam in what would become Saudi Arabia. The British, seeking to expand their influence in the Persian Gulf, signed the Anglo-Saudi Treaty in 1915, which contributed to the establishment of the Kingdom of Saudi Arabia in 1932 under King Abdulaziz, known in the West as Ibn Saud. The discovery of oil there six years later further incentivized the British and US militaries to make footprints in Saudi Arabia. With the Saudi state politically secure and Wahhabism firmly entrenched, Wahhabi religious extremism proliferated, later manifesting itself through al-Qaeda, the Taliban, and other terrorist groups.

Like Wahhabism, Shi'ite extremism is driven by modernist tendencies of institutional Islam while at the same time it is underpinned by Shi'ite enmity from wars fought against the Sunnis. Vali Nasr, a dedicated scholar with a focus on Shi'ite Islam, refers to "the old feud between Shi'ites and Sunnis" feeding Shi'ites' attitude toward Sunnis.[42] This old feud, he observes, has stirred up theological impulses that have influenced political decisions that have manifested themselves in the 1979 Iranian Revolution, the anti-Ba'thist intifada in Iraq, and the enduring conflicts in Lebanon, Syria, Saudi Arabia, Bahrain, and elsewhere. This old feud, he argues, has resulted in two separate Islams existing side by side as if in two separate states. Nasr also explains the differences as being a class distinction, with Shi'ites having become part of a middle and upper class, "educated in secular schools either in the West or at home in institutions built by European

41. Aslan, *No God but God*, 246–47; Abou El Fadl, *Great Theft*, 45–45; Delong-Bas, *Wahhabi Islam*.

42. Nasr, *Shia Revival*, 43, 82.

missionaries." This exposure, he suggests, has resulted in traditional Shi'ites becoming involved in left-wing and nationalist politics, as an alternative to the "painful question of religious identity."[43]

The contestation among jihadists as well as between extremists and reformers in Islam remains unresolved. This raises questions as to whether freedom of belief and democracy can be realistically pursued in Islam. Seen through the eyes of conservative as well as moderate Islam, Western secularism and democracy have proved through the centuries to be a failure in the world of Islam. For extremist groups, the notion of a "naked public square"—a society in which public debate is separated from reference to religious texts and values—is regarded as apostasy, leaving traditional believers alienated and offended.

The unexpected death of the Prophet in 632 CE left his companions and contemporaries in crisis. Seen as the Seal of the Prophets, Muhammad was expected to usher in the final judgment of Allah. Muhammad's death raised the question concerning who would provide a definitive interpretation of the Qur'an in the interim before Judgement Day. Differences surfaced among Muhammad's companions, divisions between Sunnis and Shi'ites tore at the unity of Islam, and disputes emerged between judicial schools. Caliphs (religious-political leaders) in turn competed to empower and control different Islamic factions, controlling their social and political agendas. The absence of the Prophet also contributed to general diversity in Islam, which continues to be heard in the voices of literalists, moderates, rationalists, modernists, and theologically progressive Islamic scholars.

Moderate Islam

Historical Islam, like Judaism, and Christianity, reflects a synthesis between the beliefs of their founding figures and the histories of their respective traditions. In Islam the primary revelation is recorded in the Qur'an and Hadith, plus the understanding of that revelation in successive generations through the 'Ulama. Probably speaking for the majority of Muslims exposed to the modern world, "traditional moderates" defend Islamic customs, practices, and primary beliefs, while seeking the deeper meaning of the Qur'an and Hadith that more conservative Muslims regard as literal truth. These moderates regard misogynist and violent commands in the Qur'an, for example, as a reflection of earlier historical contexts that can no

43. Nasr, *Shia Revival*, 82–83.

longer be accepted as the enduring teaching of Islam. They further regard theocracy and national forms of chauvinism as violations of principled Islamic inclusivity and coexistence with other faiths.[44]

The burden of moderate Muslim theologians, as in moderate Judaism and Christianity, is that although Islam is deemed unchanging and eternal throughout history, it has culturally and ethically adapted to the needs of successive generations. While some ultratraditionalists—Salafists, Wahhabis, and radical Shi'ites—have clung to what they regard as the teaching and practices of the "rightly guided" caliphs, other members of the 'Ulama in each age have adapted to the changing milieus of their time. Ebrahim Moosa, in *What is a Madrasa?*, addresses the established institution of Islamic schools, the madrassa, in south Asia, in which he addresses the needs of working-class Muslims as well as religiously minded middle classes who are troubled by the challenges that modernity presents to traditional Islamic belief. Moosa's primary critique of traditional madrassa training is directed at "rank scripturalism and toxic versions of do-it-yourself Islam that jettison tradition in order to make self-serving instruments out of tenets of faith and the teachings of scripture."[45] This, he stresses, is the brand of Islam that leads to political, tribal, and ethnic wars within Muslim states and elsewhere in the world. On a more optimistic note, he contends that it is on the "margins of the *Madrasa* tradition" that an intelligible and enlightened Islamic orthodoxy is beginning to emerge.[46]

Reza Aslan suggests that "after fourteen hundred years of rabid debate over what it means to be a Muslim . . . Islam has finally begun its fifteenth century, and with it, the realization of its own long-awaited and hard-fought Reformation."[47] Affirming the need for reform in Islam, Moosa cautions against underestimating the resistance to transformation in Islam, while identifying what he calls "unspoken and inarticulate sedimentations of different Muslim political theologies"—"active volcanoes"—that give coherence to the fragmentation within Islam.[48]

---

44. Abou El Fadl, *Great Theft*; Na'im, *Islam and Human Rights*; Na'im, *What Is an American Muslim?*

45. Moosa, *What Is a Madrasa?*, 253.

46. Moosa, *What Is a Madrasa?*, 252.

47. Aslan, *No God but God*, 277.

48. Moosa, "Political Theology in the Aftermath of the Arab Spring."

Religions of the Book

An evocative article, titled "The Muslim prophet born in Bethlehem," written by Karen Armstrong on Christmas Eve in 2006 may be a useful point of departure in such a dialogue.[49] She tells the story of Muhammad returning to Mecca in 632 CE, where he ordered the destruction of all idols and icons on the inner walls of the Ka'ba—while protecting a mural of Mary and the infant Jesus. The stories of Muhammad's partiality for the People of the Book are many.

These stories include important lessons for both Christians and Muslims. Muslims do not believe that Jesus was divine. The Qur'an sees him as a prophet, devoting more space to the miraculous conception of Jesus in the womb of Mary than does the New Testament itself, attributing his birth to the Spirit of God present in all human beings (Qur'an 19:17–29; 21:91). Armstrong reminds her fellow Christians that the Gospel writers did not believe that Jesus was God. Luke describes Jesus as a prophet, and John speaks of him as the "Word of God" rather than the essence of God.

There was close contact between Muslims and Christians during the first three hundred years of Islam. Subsequent massacres of Christians by Muslims and vice versa were largely the result of political dislocations as witnessed in the Crusades and other dark moments of history.[50] The quest for interreligious dialogue and global peace would be well served by Jews, Christians, and Muslims asking what caused the respective offspring of Abraham to earn the wrath of their cousins.[51]

49. Armstrong, "Muslim prophet born in Bethlehem."
50. Maalouf, *Crusades through Arab Eyes.*
51. Armstrong, "Muslim Prophet Born in Bethlehem."

6

Consciousness: Old and New

"When the facts change, I change my mind. What do you do, sir?"

—JOHN MAYNARD KEYNES[1]

RELIGIOUS DEBATE IS MORE nuanced than hard-line atheists give it credit for. Rudimentary fundamentalist believers, who rely on a literalist interpretation of sacred texts, exasperate as many traditional believers as they do atheists. They believe in God as a person somewhere in the heavens who controls the universe, cares for his own, and punishes the wicked. Other believers are less rigid in their convictions, giving expressions in a "non-cognitive" awareness of divine reality.[2] This involves a deeper or metaphorical understanding of the belief that God *exists*. Foundational events such as the delivery of the Ten Commandments to Moses on Mount Sinai, Jesus rising from the dead, and the literal dictation of the Qur'an to the Prophet Muhammad are understood to be representative of spiritual insights communicated through important formative myths. In addition, most believers conceivably drift between soft fundamentalism and noncognitive belief, holding their past or present religious memories in tension with modern scientific belief. This raises the question whether religion is more than habit, entrapment in outmoded practices, a passing expression of awe and wonder, intuitive engagement in pursuit of a holistic understanding of existence, or an attempt to escape the realities of earthly existence in anticipation of a

1. Words attributed to John Maynard Keynes. Quoted in Homans, "Introduction," 4.
2. Law, "Wittgenstein and Religion."

future otherworldly form of existence. The scrutiny of both atheism and religious belief identifies the multiple layers of belief present in the language of science, religion, and related disciplines.[3] The Austrian philosopher Ludwig Wittgenstein wrote, "the sole remaining task for philosophy is the analysis of language."[4] This persuades Stephen Hawking, the most inclusive and gifted of scientific theorists, to suggest that the task of science and philosophy is to discover the broad principles of a "complete theory" which "scientists, philosophers and ordinary people" can begin to understand. This, he adds, would be to "know the mind of God."[5]

The mystery of the universe and human existence is deepened and illuminated in many different images that invite us mere mortals (both empiricists and thoughtful believers) to ponder and explore the mystery of the universe, the relationship between its component parts, and our mindful selves. I suggest three images: The *Pale Blue Dot*, the emergence of the *first living cell*, and the interaction between the *neocortex and the human mind*. Reported in popular media and scholarly work, the images invite us to reach beyond what is documented or hypothesized about the unknown and the unknowable.

The "Pale Blue Dot" is captured in a photograph of planet Earth, taken by *Voyager I* on 14 February 1990 from the fringes of the solar system, some 6.4 billion kilometers away, and described by Carl Sagan in his publication *Pale Blue Dot*.[6] Planet Earth is scattered among billions of other dots of light in an arena of cosmic darkness: this picture captures the mystery of the cosmos. It includes our solar system and the sun as one of more than one hundred billion stars in a galaxy one hundred thousand light-years across, plus known and unknown galaxies, stars, and planets.[7] This picture poses the most profound set of questions ever asked. Why is there something rather than nothing? How did it all begin? Out of nothing or out of something? Who or what created it? An unmoved mover? A personal monotheistic deity? A creative source of Non-Being (as in Taoism, Hinduism, and nontheist Buddhism), or some form of eternal primeval atoms? By what criteria do some suggest that *Homo sapiens* should enjoy favor over all else on this Pale Blue Dot, tucked away in the vastness of the greater

3. Gray, *Seven Types of Atheism*.

4. Quoted in Hawking, *Brief History of Time*, 191.

5. Hawking, *Brief History of Time*, 190.

6. Sagan, *Pale Blue Dot*.

7. Shermer, "Voyager in the Cosmos."

cosmos? Creationists, theists, empiricists, evolutionists, and cosmologists offer various explanations. Some refute all contrary evidence to their own. Others offer a thoughtful, "I honestly don't know."[8]

The mystery of the first living cell, estimated to have emerged close to four billion years ago, continues to challenge the thinking of the most astute minds. Peter Folb, emeritus professor of pharmacology at the University of Cape Town and internationally renowned medical scientist, suggests, "the chances of pH [potential of hydrogen], temperature, oxygen, carbon, nitrogen, water, genetic material and gravity coming together, each in the optimum concentration [to spark life], would be infinitesimally small."[9]

Neurologists, physicists, and chemists pose related questions concerning the relationship between the physical brain and the mind in human consciousness. I go back to Francis Crick, who argued: "Your joys and sorrows, your memories and your ambitions, your sense of personal identity and free will, are in fact no more than the behavior of a vast assembly of nerve cells and their associated molecules."[10] His hypothesis that human thoughts and emotions (which include the capacity to love, an experience of awe, and psychic awareness) are no more than a consequence of the interaction of the physical brain and the human mind has since been questioned and responded to with qualifications, while his essential thesis continues to influence neuroscience.

Modern science has taken us closer to understanding the complexities of the universe, the origins of life, and the enigmas of the human mind than we have ever been before. No recognized scientist, however, claims to have the final answers to these enigmas, although some scientists argue that with the development of advanced computer algorithms this may well be possible. This could theoretically enable humans to understand and control natural laws of the universe as well as human emotions and cognitive responses to the exigencies of existence, within which computerized mathematical calculations, data processing, and automated reasoning are able to override human decision-making. The counterargument is that science and algorithms may destroy all that exists before this occurs. The "not yet known," if not the "unknowable," redefines the age-old theological

8. Shermer, "Why is There Something Rather Than Nothing?"

9. Emeritus Professor of Pharmacology at the University of Cape Town and internationally renowned medical scientist. In private conversation, June 2016.

10. Crick, *Astonishing Hypothesis*, 8.

questions: what can be said about the ineffable God of religious belief? What is a person? Who are we? Why are we here?

The God Hypothesis

The biggest challenge facing theology is the insight of neuroscience into human identity and the source of religious belief, which raises the question whether the "God hypothesis" is essentially a function of the neocortex. The standard response of theists is a pragmatic one that witnesses to the intervention and sustaining presence of a monotheistic God discerned by Jews, Christians, and Muslims over five thousand years of history.[11] This history is captured in Huston Smith's notable observation: "If we take the world's enduring religions at their best, we discover the distilled wisdom of the human race." And the extent of that wisdom continues to grow.[12]

While partisan versions of history provide valuable insights into motivation and behavior, they fall short of what Dawkins defines as "adequate [empirical] evidence" that requires the weighing of counterevidence and independent verification. Recognizing that extraordinary claims require extraordinary evidence, Dawkins was asked whether "adequate evidence" ever exists. He responded with a resolute no. The rejoinder by Michael Schermer, the editor-in-chief of *Skeptic Magazine*, is that this means that, provided we define spirituality "as a sense of awe and wonder about the grandeur of life and the cosmos," the scientific and evolutionary worldview of Dawkins "has much to offer"—presumably to the dialogue between science, the humanities, and religion. Much to the chagrin of many believers, whose knowledge of Dawkins is too often limited to his public attacks on traditional religion, Schermer satirically suggests that Dawkins should be appointed the "Skeptic's Chaplain."[13] This could go a long way to addressing the musings of progressive believers, whose "belief" goes well beyond the confines of institutional religion and dogma. If naught else, a critical understanding of spirituality could facilitate finding appropriate language to speak about a sense of "transcendent otherness" outside the confines of religious dogma. At the heart of theism is an apophatic (ineffable) sense of the divine. This places an onus on contemporary theologians to scrutinize

11. Sacks, "When Religion Goes Wrong," 251–54; Sacks, "Why God?," 268–69.

12. Moyers, *Wisdom of Faith with Huston Smith*.

13. Schermer, "Skeptic's Chaplain," 47.

sacred texts and the history of religion within the context of scientific debate and contemporary worldviews.

The origins, no less than the future, of the greater cosmos, the universe, planet Earth, and all that is within it, are regarded by the sciences to have been preceded by the big bang. Stephen Hawking formulates the problem succinctly by asking: "What is it that breathes fire into the equation that makes a universe . . ." and "Why does the universe go to all the bother of existing?"[14] Accepting that the task of science is to describe the nature of all that exists—to describe *what it is*, whereas the task of philosophers (and theologians) is to explore *why it exists*, he contends that the advances of science are such that few philosophers and others are able to understand the technical and mathematical intricacies involved. Quoting Wittgenstein, he suggests that "the sole remaining task for philosophy is the analysis of language." Recognizing the importance of language, Hawking argues that the ultimate task of science and philosophy is to discover the broad principles of a "complete theory" which "scientists, philosophers and ordinary people" can begin to understand. This, he adds, would be to "know the mind of God."[15]

Reflecting Kant's "starry heavens" as a source of ever-increasing wonder, Carl Sagan, perhaps the twentieth-century doyen of the wonders of science and cosmology in the public arena, counseled his readers (and television viewers) to "look up on a clear night," arguing that "it is very difficult to know who we are until we understand where and when we are [in the vast creative process]."[16] Despite the vast differences between science and religion, there are common threads that await a measure of confluence. The eleventh-century Benedictine monk Saint Anselm defined God as "that than which nothing greater can be conceived."[17] Descartes, Pierre Teilhard de Chardin, Alfred North Whitehead, and others subsequently probed, questioned, and modified his argument. Meanwhile, Anselm's ontological argument continues to be an ingredient in any university or seminary course on the existence of God. In continuity with select earlier philosophers and theologians, Anselm effectively transcends the populist Christian notion of God as a celestial parent or cosmic engineer who

14. Hawking, *Brief History of Time*, 190.

15. Hawking, *Brief History of Time*, 191.

16. In his 1985 Gifford Lectures, titled *Search for Who We Are*, published posthumously as Sagan, *Varieties of Scientific Experience*. Quoted in Shermer.

17. See Oppy, "Ontological Arguments."

needs to be protected from critical thought or scientific exploration. His premise continues to leave many contemporary believers with a sense of foreboding and insecurity. Fundamentalists cling to sacred texts as a source of permanence in a rapidly changing world, while many believers live with two states of consciousness—one of traditional religious belief, the other of scientific and technological conviction. Some refuse to think or speak of their doubts and uncertainties; others simply walk away from earlier beliefs, declaring themselves agnostics or atheists. As I indicated in Chapter 2, existentialists subject all philosophical, theological, and scientific attempts to critique, defining life as ultimately absurd and devoid of meaning, constituting a sense of "nothingness," which some believers and others see as a thoughtful form of spirituality.

Fast-forward: The echo of existential nothingness continues to influence theological debate. Recognizing that we are part of the greater cosmos, planet Earth, and the evolution of life, the very notion of nothingness acquires a level of theological meaning that fundamentalist religion fails to understand. Differently stated, there is a level of theological and scientific reality captured in the belief that "from nothing we have come, and to nothing we are to return." If empirically there is no evidence of something preceding the big bang and no empirical data of an "unmoved mover," then the absence of scientific data outside of physical existence is poignantly similar to what the Abrahamic faiths describe, in purely abstract and metaphorical terms, as the origin and ultimate destiny of humanity. This suggests more affinity between scientists and traditional believers than popular debate readily acknowledges.

When Facts Change

Each generation and social context generate their own way of trying to understand the source and purpose of life. Science probes, tweaks, and changes its earlier insights. Religion comes in different shapes and packages: most Jews, Christians, and Muslims embrace the broad parameters of traditional belief as a source of ethical praxis and communal accountability. Some believers, suspicious of attempts to demythologize the central events in the history of their respective faiths, reach back to a literal interpretation of scripture, which they "canonize" as an unshakable source of divine authority. Others, influenced by secular forms of self-critique and scientific literacy, live in a diverse interregnum between an inherited and an emerging notion of existence.

What is true of any knowledge-based discipline, from science to politics and economics, is true of theology. Changing perceptions of basic reality, mutating worldviews, new metaphysical insights, and the reconceptualizing of ancient truths are an inherent part of the social construction of all thought. This includes philosophy, psychology, theology, historical research, and social analysis, as well as literary and textual criticism.

The story of theology is the story of history, captured in the adage of the early Greek philosopher Heraclitus—that all is change. This explains the evolving Jewish conception of a tribal god that demands the slaughter of innocents and the annihilation of competing gods to the "reconstruction" of a single, omniscient, and omnipresent God of all humankind. Similarly, the homes of pre-Islamic tribal gods and idols in the Ka'ba shrine in Mecca were ultimately eradicated in the name of Allah.

The doctrinal impositions of traditional Judaism, Christianity, and Islam have led to internal conflict in and between these religions, which included the near extinction of the "Feminine Divine." The history of colonization is, in turn, synonymous with the destruction of indigenous beliefs in Africa, the Americas, Asia, Palestine, and elsewhere. Despite religious, gender, and racial cleansing by religious invasions and patriarchal domination over the years, indigenous theologies have regained influence in theological debate. This is seen in the revitalization of earlier beliefs, while in many Third World situations and marginalized communities elsewhere, colonial religions are increasingly being modified to incorporate both elements of indigenous beliefs and the demands of people alienated by repressive religious, economic, and political forms of domination.

Fathali Moghaddam, professor of psychology and director of the Interdisciplinary Program in Cognitive Science at Georgetown University, analyzes "ideological certainty" as a source of mutual radicalization between contemporary competing groups in conflict situations around the world. This is seen in the models of recruitment and in-group cohesion that attract those who experience injustice and relative deprivation in social structures in different ways.[18]

Preceding chapters have focused on the common origins of Judaism, Christianity, and Islam, embedded in the journey of Abram, Sarai, their offspring and followers into the unknown—plus their subsequent diverging

18. Moghaddam, *Mutual Radicalization*, 23.

paths into separate and competing religions. Entrenched in the manipulation of theological and ideological memories and historical developments, these faiths have come to symbolize the hostility embedded in current global politics, while progressive believers see no good reason for Jews, Christians, and Muslims to surrender to their historic identities. In the words of Saint Bernard of Clairvaux, "We all drink from our own wells."[19]

This anticipates two alternatives: A negative reaction to issues of social identity (including gender, sexual, economic, and racial priorities) that could result in further fragmentation within the Abrahamic faiths. More positively, a negative reaction to finding identity could persuade religious communities to embrace diversity and religious pluralism. Both options provide doctrinal, ethical, and ritualistic challenges that could change the face of religion in the West, not merely as a result of abstractions and debate, but primarily as a result of contextual social experience. These could result from globalization, multiculturalism, and changing economic circumstances, as well as from increased exposure to the sciences on the functioning of the universe, the insights of neuroscience about religious belief, and psychological analyses on the source of violence and religious conflict. The propensity of humanity to commit atrocities is a given reality. History also shows that *Homo sapiens* (perhaps because of the will to survive) are adaptive, creative, and imaginative creatures. The challenge is to harness all available human resources to explore the underlying roots of domestic violence, hate crimes, and the slaughter of people who are seen to be different, as well as the sense of impotence and indifference by perhaps the majority of people to allow this to happen.

Abu Hamid al-Ghazali (c. 1058–1111), the prominent Islamic scholar in the eleventh and twelfth centuries (discussed in Chapter 5), likened the search for integrous faith to "a deep ocean strewn with shipwrecks," warning that once "blind faith" is abandoned it is impossible to again believe. To quote Ghazali, "Like shattered glass, the fragments cannot be recovered, except by being cast again into the furnace and refashioned."[20] This is precisely what he did. Having transgressed the limits of orthodox belief, he took it upon himself to recast his shattered faith by establishing a middle ground between "blind faith" and the rational challenges embedded in a "deep ocean." In sum,

19. In Tayob, *Journey through Critical and Philosophical Reconstructions of Islam* (unpublished manuscript); see also Gutiérrez, *We Drink from Our Own Wells*.

20. In Tayob, *Journey through Critical and Philosophical Reconstructions of Islam* (unpublished manuscript); see also Moosa, *Ghazali and the Poetics of Imagination*, 260–61.

he argued that doubt is part of the journey to truth. It opens the way to new insights. "Who does not doubt, does not look [search]. And who does not look, does not perceive. And who does not perceive stays in blindness and error from which we seek refuge from God."[21]

Blind faith as well as the comforts of a cultural, emotional, and religious home cannot easily be cast aside. Yet there are some who find the very meaning of life for which they search beyond the confines of a familial or religious home. Ready to explore the boundaries of an inherited faith, they find a new home through the very doubt and questions they feared most in the depths of the ocean. It is here, amid the "unknowable" dimensions of life, that they find a sense of "restless comfort."[22] In contemporary society this is found in dialogue with the natural scientists, neurologists, and social scientists and in the study of the humanities, which comes ever closer to the existential ground once owned by religion. This is an ownership that religion has relinquished with hesitation and sometimes with a fight.

While ultimately adapting to changing worldviews, the resistance to the modern scientific revolution in the seventeenth century was of a different kind. At the risk of overemphasis, the hypotheses and theories from mathematicians, physicists, and astronomers challenged the very foundations of religious belief. A primary figure was René Descartes (1596–1650). Regarded as the father of modern philosophy, he evoked the wrath of church leaders for his critique of scholastic theology, while defending himself as a member of the Catholic Church, offering what he saw as an ontological argument for the existence of God as a perfect being. He argued that all else (in theology, science, and philosophy) needed to be regarded as open to debate and to rejection if it induced the slightest doubt. Other formative figures in the scientific age included Isaac Newton (1643–1727), whose laws of motion challenged established theology, while at times they were used to explain the biblical beliefs in creation. The books of Nicolaus Copernicus (1473–1543) were banned in 1616, and Galileo Galilei (1564–1642) was condemned by the Roman Catholic Inquisition in 1633. (The restrictions on Copernicus were lifted in the nineteenth century, and formal condemnation of Galileo was not expunged until 1992.)

The eighteenth-century Enlightenment had in the interim impacted significantly on theological and philosophical debate, resulting in an

21. Quotations from Tayob, *Journey through Critical and Philosophical Reconstructions of Islam*, 255–60. See also Moosa, *Ghazali and the Poetics of Imagination*, 93–119.

22. See Barrow, "Unknowable Unknowns."

openness to science and the influence of secularism in the Judeo-Christian tradition.[23] Several leading Jewish scholars associate the insights of Darwin's biology and recent developments in science with key ideas in the Bible.[24] Christian believers and theologians are among the most positive and formative thinkers in the promotion of the science and religion debate. Viewed largely as a Western phenomenon, secularism (rather than science per se) has conversely come to be negatively viewed in institutional Islam. Despite the heritage of Ibn Rushd and others in the twelfth-century renaissance, the impact of the natural sciences has at the same time presented its own set of challenges to traditional forms of Islamic beliefs and practices.

The Neuroscientific Revolution

Neuroscience tells us that humans have two brains: The limbic system or primal brain, consists of a complex system of nerves, nuclei, and tracts that control the basic drives for food and sex, for submission, dominance, anger, and pleasure in both animals and humans. The neocortex or new brain subsequently developed in higher mammals and approximately two hundred thousand years ago evolved into the human brain. Consisting of over a billion neurons and several billion synapses, the human neocortex responds to events in thoughtful and analytical ways that separate *Homo sapiens* from earlier hominids. These responses include curiosity, imagination, and thoughtfulness, which arguably lead humans to seek new knowledge, ask metaphysical questions, and probe the sources of technical innovation and development.

Francis Crick's views are central to functional Magnetic Resonance Imaging (fMRI) in neuroscience, initiated in the 1990s.[25] The research of Evan Thompson, a cognitive scientist at the University of British Columbia, portrays human consciousness as a complex, fluctuating relationship between brain and the mind; Thompson argues that a person's electrophysical brain patterns are significantly influenced by mindful social and intellectual activity and exposure, while the physiology of the brain remains paramount.[26] The field-based interviews and laboratory-based research of Richard Davidson, professor of psychology and psychiatry at the University

23. Asad, *Formations of the Secular*.

24. Sacks, "Darwin."

25. Scruton, "Neurononsense and the Soul."

26. Valera et al., *Embodied Mind*, 98–99.

of Wisconsin–Madison, similarly map a link between emotional behavior and the physical brain, a connection embedded in the animals of the field and hominids.[27] Yuval Harari is persuaded that neuroscience is key to understanding human decision-making—from mundane decision-making to decision-making that shapes human nature in relation to the universe.[28] Reza Aslan similarly argues that the human propensity to ascribe to other humans agency for events that happen in their environment is a "biological process that arose deep in our evolutionary past," and that "*every impulse without exception* is generated by complex electrochemical reactions in the brain." These include religious impulses or experiences, which, like romantic attractions, do not make the object of these impulses any less real or less worthy.[29] The widespread nature of such impulses, suggests that the human quest to transcend one's individual or personal existence is an inherent part of human consciousness.

These and related insights thrust progressive theologians into debate on whether humans have any sense of free will at all. On the one side is the contention that free will is the result of the unconscious brain-state, which raises the normative moral question as to whether a person has any capacity to control his or her essential decisions in life. On the other side, it is argued that a person is part of a social and intellectual environment that impacts on the synapses of the physical brain.[30] (Existentialist *âmes sœurs*, Sartre, Camus, and Simone de Beauvoir dismissed the free-will-versus-determinism debate, simply resolving that existence precedes essence.) Writing in the *New Yorker*, Gary Marcus, a professor of psychology at New York University, argued that "The idea that the mind can be separated from the brain no longer makes sense. They are simply different ways of describing the same thing," suggesting that to talk about the brain is to talk about physiology, neurons, receptors, and neurotransmitters and to talk about the mind is to talk about thoughts, ideas, beliefs, emotions, and desires. "The 'mind'" he says, "is what the brain does," which suggests that the choice of neuroscience is not between the brain and the mind, it is to build bridges between the two.[31]

27. Davidson and Begley, *Emotional Life of Your Brain*.

28. Harari, "Work."

29. Aslan, *God: A Human History*, 38 (italics original).

30. Satel and Lilienfeld, *Brainwashed*; Malik, *Quest for a Moral Compass*; Barton, *Skeptic's Guide to the Mind*;

31. Marcus, "Problem with the Neuroscience Backlash."

Exposed to these and related insights of neuroscience, thoughtful believers are confronted with the question whether religion may be no more than a function of the engagement between the brain and mind. Within this context, Robert Wright's *The Evolution of God* has attracted popular and scholarly attention. He argues that religion, like public morality, is a slow, contested, and inconclusive process. He attributes the current monotheism of the Abrahamic faiths to early forms of animism, war gods, and creator gods that "evolved" into a spiritual perception of an all-purpose God and, over the millennia, into a more compassionate God as portrayed in current manifestations of mainstream Abrahamic religions.[32]

Robert Wright argues that this is not primarily because of some psychological need for a God of human kindness, but the result of a maturing capacity of different groups to coexist (largely out of self-interest). Yet he shows that when individuals, groups, and nations are under threat, they reconceptualize God as a partisan God of revenge and slaughter. Wright, at the same time, marvels at the remarkable biological evolution of humans in a world and universe born out of subatomic particles, and the material emergence of water, rocks, and land and then fish, reptiles, and different forms of mammals. He argues that despite the limitations and failures of humanity, plus the distinct possibility of a human-generated extinction of the planet, the "manifest existence of a moral order" is what "makes it reasonable" for believers to suspect there is some basis for speaking of a "higher purpose in life that qualifies for the label 'god' in at least some sense of that word." He, at the same time, argues that transcendence is "a very tricky word . . . spooky, mystical, ethereal stuff," which he concludes is beyond his comprehension.[33]

Paul Bloom, a leading psychologist at Yale University, refers to Wright's *The Evolution of God* as a "brilliant new book" in which Wright explains the wonders of a universe that gave rise to mentally and morally enriched beings, contending that the idea of God is somewhere between "illusion and imperfect conception." Wright further argues that even if human progress could be attributed to a God of love, this would be a "terribly minimalist God," who fails to answer prayer or smite enemies, which Wright argues is not the kind of God for which most believers are looking.[34]

---

32. Wright, *Evolution of God*, 4, 460–61; see also Wright, *Nonzero*.

33. Moyers, Interview with Robert Wright.

34. Bloom, "No Smiting."

John de Gruchy, a deeply committed Christian believer and progressive theologian, offers a more nuanced understanding of God. He reclaims the often-neglected theological notion of the soul, which is traditionally defined as "an immortal, divine and discrete essence in each individual." In contrast to the imagery seen in Gilbert Ryle's "Ghost in the Machine" (and aspects of traditional theology), de Gruchy describes the soul as a symbol of the "complex, dynamic and relational" aspect of the psychosomatic wholeness of humanity. As such, the soul is *who* I am, and *who* I am becoming, in myself and in my relationships. So de Gruchy understands the soul not as a detached, disembodied, and discrete entity, but as the symbol of who I am and who I am becoming in the totality of my existence. The significance in using the word *soul* is that it suggests that at the center of humanity is an awareness of cosmic reality and capacity to be open to the transcendent or what theistic religions refer to as God.[35]

Situated within the apophatic theological paradigm, de Gruchy's theology reflects the major tenets of monotheistic belief, which include a "sacred space" within which humans are able to encounter ultimate reality or a sense of divine transcendence. Traversing the border between theology and neuroscience, de Gruchy explores the interrelationship between the neurology of the human brain and the more abstract human mind, drawing on the psychiatric and neuroimaging research of Iain McGilchrist and other neurologists concerning the manner in which the left and right sides of the brain impact on the mind. Embracing the philosophical insights of Keith Ward, de Gruchy explores the theological implications of the right hemisphere of the brain, which is generally regarded as responsible for the emotional and intuitive dimensions of human consciousness and is often overlooked in an age that prioritizes reason and logic in the promotion of science, mathematics, and technology.[36]

Both McGilchrist and Ward are partial to religious and specifically Christian theological constructs of human identity. McGilchrist opines that any mythology that explores the spiritual order, giving us something other than material values to live by, "is more valuable than one that dismisses the possibility of its existence."[37] Ward argues that the mind "is not a separate hidden world connected arbitrarily to the body" but "a realm of partly unverifiable privately accessed data" that includes a "rich,

35. De Gruchy, "Retrieving the Soul."
36. McGilchrist, *Master and His Emissary*; Ward, *More Than Matter?*
37. McGilchrist, *Master and His Emissary*, 442.

value-filled complex entity of feelings, thought, and intentions," which is a key element of human existence. For Ward, the mind is "embedded in" and "emerges from" the physical matter of the brain but can "in principle be decoupled from matter." For him, this means "the brain state and the mental state are not strictly identical."[38]

As more are exposed to these and similar insights of neuroscience, a growing number of discerning people are becoming increasingly critical of traditional religious beliefs while also demonstrating an apparent intuitive impulse to probe social and metaphysical reality beyond ourselves—whether unknown or unknowable. This harks back to the early Jewish belief that the name of this impulse, which would evolve into monotheistic belief, is beyond words or conceptualization. For devout mystics the sacred Tetragrammaton YHWH cannot be pronounced. Like air it can only be breathed. Drawing on this tradition, it is suggested: "YH on the inbreath and WH on the outbreath." Determined to replace the dignity of silence, Christianity contributes enduring religious conflict. Often overlooked in the West, Jewish Kabbalist and Islamic Sufi spirituality includes silence as an expression of the unknown divine, often ignored in Christian exclusivity.

Frequently adopting a cautious and respectful response to their personal and ancestral beliefs, thoughtful believers tone down the harsher dimensions embedded in the Abrahamic religious traditions, while affirming three minimal theological and ethical principles: *the recognition and presence of a transcendent God in all that exists, the dignity and love of others, and respect for the planet Earth and cosmic order.* This God is seen as a God of history, made known in all creation, in special revelatory events, and the source of existential meaning traceable back over five thousand years. This suggests a space within a viable conversation between science and religion that correlates with the work of Wentzel van Huyssteen, E. O. Wilson, and others. The theological constructs of such writers are vastly different from those of religious fundamentalists, who cling to scriptural literalism and dogmatic belief while resisting interfaith and interdisciplinary discussion.

Neuroscience directly and by implication has emerged as the major architect of an emerging new understanding of human existence. The evolution of ideas and beliefs is, however, a slow (and tedious) process, invariably accompanied by resistance that is influenced perhaps more by emotions than by rational thought. Entrenched ideas protect us from opposing insights that are uncomfortable and disruptive of our complacency and often of our status

38. Ward, *More Than Matter?*, 112–16 (italics added).

in life. This resistance aside, the rational critique of dominant thinking has relentlessly challenged prevailing ideas in each age.

The dialogical encounter between science and religion has clearly moved beyond the tired debate on the factual veracity of the Genesis story of creation, the material legitimacy of the story of Moses and the burning bush, whether Jesus really walked on water, or whether there is empirical evidence of the archangel Gabriel having instructed the illiterate Prophet Muhammad to read. Religion is about more than a collection of miraculous events or subjective experiences. To the extent that scientists and theologians are both committed to truth-seeking, dialogue holds the potential for mutual enrichment.

The New Dialectic

Judaism, Christianity, and Islam share a single theological feature, which is an ineffable or apophatic belief that God is beyond human capacity to describe, define, or understand. This age-old theological principle, often forgotten in popular religion, constitutes an insight that deserves renewed prominence in the dialogue between science and religion, as well as in the politics of regional, national, and global conflict. Apophatic theology suggests a humility that undermines both implied and explicit forms of theocracy.

Some fundamentalists interpret allegories and parables as historical truth. Other believers have through the ages sought to discern the deeper meanings captured in traditional metaphors, myths, and stories, as well as to recognize the limitations of the language and the semantics of creeds and sacred memories. Different ways of interpreting sacred events have led to theological disputes, and probes into the scientific accounts of the origins of the universe and planet Earth; not to mention investigations into the limitations of empiricism and the constraints of analytical philosophy; finally different ways of interpreting sacred events also color the pretentious rhetoric of preachers who proclaim privileged insights into the being and dictates of God.

Chapter 1 noted that Sean Carroll, a leading theoretical scientist, embraces Muriel Rukeyser's poetic argument that "the universe is made of stories, not atoms."[39] Carroll encourages poets, novelists, theologians, and others to share their stories, myths, and reflections on the origins and

39. Carroll, *Big Picture*, 19.

ultimate questions about life and the purpose of life in heartfelt imagination. For him there is one proviso: These stories need to be "compatible
with modern physics," increasingly regarded as the most convincing and
logical explanation of planet Earth and all within it.[40] Most thoughtful people and open-minded theologians scarcely disagree with Carroll's proviso.
A refusal to do so raises the question as to whether religion can meaning-
fully participate in contemporary debate driven by science. Returning to
Hawking, science addresses *what*, philosophy *why*.

Rethinking Religion

In his satirical essay "Memorial Service for Dead Gods," the early twentieth-century literary critic and writer H. L. Mencken provides a classic
list of dead gods: "Where is the graveyard of dead gods?" he asks. "What
lingering mourner waters their mounds?" He suggests that there was "a
time when Jupiter was the king of the gods, and anyone who doubted his
puissance was regarded as a barbarian and ignoramus." Mencken then
goes further. He suggests that the dogma and uncritical submission of
loyal worshipers brought destruction on the worshipers themselves and
their gods (Jupiter, Zeus, Thor, Baal, and others), so that ultimately these
divinities were assigned to the panoply of dead gods.[41] New religions
came to be discerned in the consciousness of the West: Eastern, Asian,
African, Third World, and theist, including an array of Christian splinter
groups. These new religions elevated transcendence and immanence, as
well as personal and impersonal levels of the inner self, the presence of
supernatural realities, divinities, and ultimate reality. The list is endless,
embracing Aztec, Maya, Yoruba, Khoisan, Bantu, Asian, and Eastern dei-
ties. The realization and importance of religious and cultural pluralism is
still in its infancy among adherents of the major Abrahamic faiths. Many
devout believers (not least Christians and Muslims) regard followers of
other faiths to be targets of proselytization.

All historical evidence shows that traditions and cultures evolve and
change. This realization is developed (some would say exploited) in post-
modernist thought. Ian Almond compares the great twelfth- and thirteenth-
century Sufi spiritual leader Ibn 'Arabi's sense of spiritual "bewilderment"

40. Carroll, *Big Picture*, 19. See also National Geographic Society, "Map of Human
Migration."

41. Mencken, "Memorial Service."

or "perplexity" (*hayrah*) to that of Jacques Derrida's (1930–2004) postmodern deconstructuralism, within which Derrida adopted an anti-Platonic reading of a "text" in literature, the visual arts, philosophy, and elsewhere.[42] At the risk of simplification (and he encouraged devious thinking), he rejected the possibility of an original text, searching for variation, difference, playfulness and, where appropriate, "anarchy" in debate, in search of what he called the "*Real*" or "*tout autre*" (total otherness).[43] Derrida read and reread Marx, Sartre, and the foundational texts of Judaism and Christianity. He rejected convention in the search of the Other. Ian Almond compares Derrida's Other with Ibn 'Arabi Allah's focus on Allah as "wholly Other, beyond comprehension, imagination or definition" and yet deeply personal.[44] For Derrida, the search for the Real is a transformative process that recognizes the changing nature of the text and a "metaphysics of presence."[45] Effectively, his counsel was to read a text, reflect on it, inwardly digest it, and question the exigencies of contemporary existence, exposing it to past and future interpretation. For him, the text belongs both to its scribe and to each successive reader.

Ibn 'Arabi's twelfth-century mysticism and Derrida's contemporary literary hermeneutics remind us of the multiplicities in the history of religion being more than the preservation of an archaeological relic, sacred interpretation, protected memory, or product of arid textual exegesis. In the prophetic words of Jeremiah (2:13; 17:13), organic religion is "living water" in the form of the struggle for social justice, the empowerment of the poor, the exposure of class-based rights, and the humanization of others, as captured in liberation theology that exposes discrimination on the basis of race, gender, and religion. Rejecting the stubborn dictates of restrictive forms of fundamentalism as well as the suffocation of twentieth-century European textual criticism, Derrida seeks to uncover a sense of mystery in the metaphorical and poetic insights of the ages through new ways of understanding ancient truths that he accuses free-thinking atheists of overlooking.

The more theology changes and is rejected, the more the questions identified by paleontologists and the fragments of the historical record

42. Derrida, "'This Strange Institution Called Literature.'"

43. Almond, "Honesty of the Perplexed"; Attridge and Baldwin, "Jacques Derrida" (obituary).

44. Almond, "Honesty of the Perplexed."

45. Attridge and Baldwin, "Jacques Derrida" (obituary).

seem to be explored in new ways. This is seen in the rediscovery of Eastern and Asian religious ideas, and of indigenous religions in Africa and in North and South America. But religious ideas are not the only ones that have been rediscovered: consider Freudian unconsciousness, Jungian collective unconsciousness, Marxist materialism, philosophical metaphysics, and the projections of artificial intelligence. No one size fits all.

There is a growing consensus among progressive theologians in nearly all major religions that the quest for holistic truth needs to be located in what Steven Pinker refers to as an interconnected sense of reality that he calls a "multiverse," "comprising everything" from the birds, bees, animals of the field, and ecology to the entirety of space, matter, energy, and the laws of nature.[46] The playful rejection of the "simplicity" of God, suggested by Jacques Derrida and deconstructuralists, including the Jewish sage Emmanuel Levinas, and Michel Foucault, stretches the minds of traditionalists and contributes to the detection of toxic forms of patriarchy, racism, and related obsolete impositions on human consciousness and religion.

Cut to the core, the history of religion makes a modest contribution to efforts to understand the mysteries of life preserved in myth, memory, meme, metaphor, imagination, and time-bound assumptions. Theology is, at best, as wide and inclusive as human conception allows, drawing on science, religious traditions, the humanities, and social sciences, plus creative hunches that believers and nonbelievers find difficult to conceptualize. Humans are a curious, thoughtful, visionary, and creative species who have through trial, error, success, and dismal failure contributed to the perception of marvels in the modern world. Humans are also a source of egotistical self-indulgence, rivalry, hegemonic control, and slaughter that leave a negative imprint on existence.

Despite visions of a global village, the reality is that this village continues to be torn apart by economic rivalry and struggles for political hegemony supported by the interests of cultural and religious factions that operate under the façade of what Freud described as the "narcissism of minor differences"—differences that lure simple believers into complex politicoreligious alliances.[47] While the history of Judaism, Christianity, and Islam is rooted in the tension between text and interpretation, underpinned by the complexities of creedal and jurisprudential decrees, the broad principles of the

46. Pinker, *Enlightenment Now*, 410–53; see de Gruchy, *Confessions of a Christian Humanist*.

47. Marshall, *Divided*.

Abrahamic faiths are supported both by many thoughtful believers within institutional religions and by the broader civil society of both believers and nonbelievers. These principles are supported by theologians familiar with ancient philosophies and the history of theological debate as well as by many secularist scholars. These include secular poets, writers of fiction, and iconoclasts who influence the broader population of grassroots and professional people, many of whom have neither the time nor the desire to address the existential meaning inherent to Judeo-Christian-Islamic belief.

Recognizing the primary or special revelation of God to Jews in the Law and the Prophets, the self-revelation of God in the person of Jesus Christ, and the Prophet Muhammad through the Qur'an, the Abrahamic faiths at the same time recognize universal or general revelation. The recognition is that no person or community is excluded from God's revelation and presence as they are communicated in the natural order, in the human quest for meaning, in philosophy, community building, and moral endeavors. There is Elijah's recognition of the "still small voice" and a "cloud the size of the human hand" (1 Kgs 19:11–12; 18:44) as well as Jesus' parables told for those who "listen but never understand . . . or perceive" (Mark 4:10–13). Ghazali's counsel is to discern Allah's presence in the challenges of the deepest ocean, recognizing that "who does not perceive stays in blindness and error," contending that Allah *is* the light that enables us to discern the truth in all that is in heaven and earth.[48]

Despite the creativity and adventurous spirits that separated early humans from their hominid ancestors, the story of conscious human adaptation and material development included anxieties, challenges and fears. For millennia, humans have been reared, socialized, and indoctrinated in traditional societies, with a sense of the mystical presence of spirits and ancestors, and with the security of religious rites—but in rejecting the mystical, secularization challenges the depths of human identity and belonging. It reduces life to the limitations of reason, logic, and empiricism, leaving custom, belonging, and emotion unexplained. Rationalists, existentialists, and responding theologians (discussed in Chapter 2) and subsequent forms of scholarship have struggled to make sense of the challenge of living with secularization. Increased secularization has accentuated the importance of traditional and contextually significant historical novels, poetry, and memes and adapted memories, renewed forms of consciousness and awareness,

48. Ghazali quoted in Tayob, *Journey through Critical and Philosophical Reconstructions of Islam.*

that have a capacity to speak and be heard where the transcendent dimension of traditional religion is unheard by all but the trained ears of the most devout believers. The parallel between this genre of literature and the parables and images inherent in the sacred texts of the Judeo-Christian and Islamic traditions is, from a pastoral if not theological perspective, an ingredient that the protectors of traditional dogma would do well to ponder. Truth, spiritual awareness, and invitation to see, hear, and understand in the "deepest ocean" and "shattered glass" of blind faith is vividly portrayed in Abu al-Ghazali's quest for meaning and belief.

Twelfth-century Iberian rationalists employed Greek philosophy and allegorical exegesis in debate, as seen in the theology of Ghazali, Averroes, Maimonides, and Thomas Aquinas, as well as in the response of Ibn 'Arabi and Rūmī in the Sufi tradition to the rationalism that impacted on scholasticism across Europe. The objective of these theologies is captured in Saint Anselm, the archbishop of Canterbury's, *Credo ut intelligum* ("I believe so that I may understand"), which led to a dialogue with the nominalist philosopher and theologian Peter Abelard, who insisted that the first step towards true belief is diligent and persistent questioning. Abelard drew on unrelenting logic and philosophy to probe the doctrine of the church. He affirmed the basic principles of established Christian doctrine, ritual, and devotion, while rejecting the belief that only a Christian could be saved, saying that heretics should be constrained by reason, not force. His teaching was condemned by Pope Innocent II in 1140, and Abelard took refuge in the monastery of Cluny under the protection of Peter the Venerable, where he died in obscurity.

Doubt and Imagination

Dogmatic and entrenched believers often hold a conviction that it is improper to acknowledge doubt or think again about the unknown realities of their existence. By contrast, thoughtful observers, marginalized believers, open-minded secularists, and nondogmatic agnostics cultivate an openness to experience the mystery that encapsulates the defeats and victories of history past, the transient nature of the present, and the lure of unknown future.

The South African novelist Zakes Mda finds the wellspring of life's meaning in the landscape of his ancestral home. In an essay titled "The Pink Mountain," he reflects on the natural beauty of the mountains surrounding

Qoboshane, where his ancestors lived in the Eastern Cape. Looking beyond "the ordinary," he suggests "place" has a capacity to draw us out of our "self-centeredness" back into continuity with earlier generations and nature itself. In a Zen-like manner, he becomes conscious of himself, not in isolation from but in continuity with his ancestral community "memorialized and alchemized . . . in frozen rituals on cave walls," with Bushmen (or San people) who once populated the area.[49] In a separate essay subtitled "An Outsider's Reflections on Place, Memory and the Creative Process," Mda tells of his visit, as a stranger, to Wayne National Forest in Ohio in the United States. Having contemplated the tranquil beauty of the forested hills, he reflects on the "mythic memory" of Native Americans and slaves, the ramshackle remnants of a deserted coal mining town, and the later German and Irish indentured workers who found refuge in what he calls a historical confluence of "White, Indian and Negro" people. He sees life as a sequential and elusive journey that includes an imaginary journey into the past and a projection into the unknown future.[50]

In a classic poem, Emily Dickinson suggested that "truth must dazzle gradually . . . or every man [would] be blind." Reflecting perhaps her own social and religious milieu, she said, tell it "slant," tell it "eased" or "kindly as if explaining lightning and thunderstorms to a child."[51] Zealous preachers and impulsive politicians, as well as impulsive aspirant scientific initiates, are usually less restrained. They tell it bluntly, habitually refusing to take a second look at their own certainty and intractable opinion. Truth is multifaceted, elusive, and difficult to communicate—even without being subjected to banter, confrontation, and violence. Life's meaning and purpose is deeply personal and communal, discerned through the natural, reflective, intellective, and artistic inquiry that goes well beyond formal religion. This is reflected in Barbara Tuchman's *The March of Folly,* which refers to the "mythical truths" that recur as "throughout history, regardless of place and period." Refusing to offer any explanation for the enigmas of life, she lures her readers into pondering the nature of moral truths in the human struggle for survival and dominance.[52] She suggests that human decision-making, wise and foolish, simply cannot be reduced to conclusive physical, political, or social analyses. For her, there is invariably more to be pondered but

49. Mda, *Justify the Enemy,* 30–40.
50. Mda, *Justify the Enemy,* 72–78.
51. Tearle, "Short Analysis."
52. Tuchman, *March of Folly,* 2–4.

not explained. Joyce Carol Oates, a leading contemporary American literary author and humanist, discerns the deep need for meaning as being inherent to humanity. Written in a different genre from Tuchman's work, Oates's fiction and poetry capture what she defines as "the human spirit yearning to transcend the merely finite and ephemeral to participate in something mysterious and communal called culture."[53] She argues that thoughtful people instinctively explore the anomalies of life, whether through creative thinking, speculation, myth, memory and storytelling, art, or music. This, she suggests, leaves the artist "born damned," needing to struggle through life with a sense of incompleteness, driven by a sense of inadequacy in pursuit of "complete redemption."[54] Story and nuance is often heard by the uninitiated and doubtful believer more clearly than dogma.

Spiritual Bandwidth

These stories tell us life has its surprises. They also tell us that everything in life is connected. What we sow somebody reaps. We cannot simply be fruitful and multiply, fill the earth and subdue it, claiming dominion over the fish of the sea and over the birds of the air and over every living thing that moves upon the earth (Gen 1:28). We are a transient and miniscule instance on a blue dot in a vast cosmic arena; there is an inherent link between the first single living cell to emerge and the entire universe and, conceivably, the only self-conscious hominids in existence. This gives us a special responsibility regarding the universe, which we have abused. Religion both reminds us of these truths and demonstrates the manner in which our theological constructs have often been manipulated to disregard these truths.

Richard Rohr, whose thought, rather than his remarkable spiritual discipline, is implicit in the pages of this and earlier chapters, reflects "alternative orthodoxy" as a substitute for rigid forms of orthodox belief, shifting the focus of faith from "black and white, good and bad" and aggravations that characterize the minutiae of religious dogma to a broader exploration of the cosmos, the ecological order, and the depths of what it means to be human.[55] This enlarged bandwidth locates the ineffable (apophatic) mystery of life in an all-encompassing quest for truth that includes the biological, natural, and neurological sciences; the history of world religions; and fiction

53. Oates, *Faith of a Writer*, 94.
54. Oates, *Faith of a Writer*, 41.
55. Rohr, "Many Ways of Knowing."

and poetry that gives expression to the imagination of different cultures, religions, and tribes. An enlarged spiritual bandwidth extends the notion of belief from a rational endeavor to understand and emotional dependency to orthopraxis and sacred activism, which is included in the teaching of the world's great religions.[56] A spiritual and meticulous scholar, Rohr embraces cognitive debate, the philological roots of sacred texts, and the nature of scientific method, contending that conventional religion has narrowed its existential focus to the point of creedal and jurisprudential obscurity. This, he argues, is at the cost of the inherent width and depth of thoughtful human consciousness. He argues that as this awareness unfolds, institutional religion is likely to undergo a "Copernican revolution."[57]

Frank Close, Oxford University professor of physics, reminds us that "with each breath, we inhale a million billion atoms of oxygen, which gives some idea of how small each atom is. All of them, together with the carbon atoms in your skin, and indeed everything else on Earth, were cooked in a star some five billion years ago. So you are made of stuff that is as old as the planet, one-third as old as the universe, though this is the first time that those atoms have been gathered together such that they think that they are you."[58] This suggests there is a certain permanence about us. There is no empirical evidence that the accumulated atoms that constitute a given person will do other than dissipate at the time of our physical death, being reabsorbed into the greater universe. This gives some credence to the popular Eastern spiritual ideas that people are passing manifestations of the universe. (My twelve-year-old grandson and I were engaged in discussion of these matters. Facing the finitude of human life, he said, "Well, I suppose we will simply be recycled.")

Broadband spirituality, as expressed by Rohr and an increasing number of believers who feel inherently restricted by institutional forms of dogma and control, goes well beyond the confines of religion. It is as much an ethic as a belief. It is epistemology, involving the *manner* in which we see, hear, and try to understand the greater universe and our limited but important role within it. It involves a realization that who we are is a gift to us from the ecological environment, the positive advances of science and modern technology, and the inheritance and affirmation of a set of shared ethical values. Practicing broadband spirituality further

56. See Rohr, "Many Ways of Knowing"; Rohr, "Franciscan Way."
57. Rohr, "Evidence-Based Emergence."
58. Close, *Particle Physics*.

involves acknowledging the fragile nature of what constitutes humanity and planetary survival. Metaphysical and theological debate; the natural, behavioral, and neurological and social sciences; plus the imagination and provocation of the arts all contribute to the human quest for understanding life. Spirituality contains one further reality, which includes a sense of what is unknowable. Maybe the essence of humanity includes an entrenched quest for certainty, whereas thoughtfulness includes an inevitable measure of uncertainty. Others, to abuse the words of Stephen Hawking, pretend they know the mind of God.

Bibliography

Abou El Fadl, Khaled. *The Great Theft: Wrestling Islam from the Extremists*. San Francisco: HarperSanFrancisco, 2005.

Almond, Ian. "The Honesty of the Perplexed: Derrida and Ibn 'Arabi on 'Bewilderment.'" *Journal of the American Academy of Religion* 70 (2002) 515–37.

Appiah, Kwame Anthony. *The Lies That Bind: Rethinking Identity*. New York: Liveright, 2018.

Appleby, Scott. *The Ambivalence of the Sacred: Religion, Violence, and Reconciliation*. Lanham, MD: Rowman & Littlefield, 2000.

Armstrong, Karen. *The Case for God*. New York: Knopf, 2009.

———. *Fields of Blood: Religion and the History of Violence*. New York: Knopf, 2014.

———. "The Muslim Prophet Born in Bethlehem." Opinion. Religion. *Guardian*, December 23, 2006. https://www.theguardian.com/commentisfree/2006/dec/23/religion.christmas

Asad, Talal. *Formations of the Secular: Christianity, Islam, Modernity*. Cultural Memory in the Present. Stanford: Stanford University Press, 2003.

Aslan, Reza. *Beyond Fundamentalism: Confronting Extremism in the Age of Globalization*. New York: Random House, 2010.

———. *God: A Human History*. New York: Random House, 2017.

———. *No God but God: The Origins, Evolution and Future of Islam*. New York: Random House, 2011.

Atkins, Kim. "Paul Ricoeur (1913–2005)." *Internet Encyclopedia of Philosophy*. https://www.iep.utm.edu/ricoeur/.

Attridge, Derek, and Thomas Baldwin. "Jacques Derrida: The Meaning of Language and Aesthetic Values." *Guardian*, October 11, 2004. https://www.theguardian.com/news/2004/oct/11/guardianobituaries.france.

Bacon, Francis. *Essays, Civil and Moral*. First published 1597. http://www.gutenberg.org/ebooks/575.

Baldwin, James. "Unnameable Objects, Unspeakable Crimes." In *The White Problem in America*, 173–81. Chicago: Johnson, 1966. See also https://blackstate.com/james-baldwin-unnameable-objects-unspeakable-crimes.

Barrow, John H. "Unknowable Unknowns." Keynote lecture presented at the 38th Social Research Conference at the New School for Social Research, New York City (in conversation with Rebecca Goldstein). April 4, 2019. https://www. centerforpublicscholarship.org/single-post/2019/01/10/Unknowability-How-Do-We-Know-What-Cannot-Be-Known.

Barton, Robert A. *A Skeptic's Guide to the Mind: What Neuroscience Can and Cannot Tell Us about Ourselves.* New York: St. Martin's Griffin, 2014.

Battenhouse, R. W., ed. *A Companion to the Study of St. Augustine.* Grand Rapids: Baker, 1969.

Beard, Mary. *SPQR: A History of Ancient Rome.* London: Profile Books, 2016.

Bigongiari, Dino, ed. *The Political Ideas of St. Thomas Aquinas.* New York: Hafner, 1969.

Bin Laden, Osama. "Declaration of Jihad against Jews and Crusaders." In *The Theory and Practice of Islamic Terrorism: An Anthology,* edited by Marvin Perry and Howard E. Negrin, 140–47. New York: Palgrave Macmillan, 2008.

Blackmore, Susan J. *The Meme Machine.* Popular Science. New York: Oxford University Press, 1999.

Bloom, Harold. *The Flight to Lucifer.* New York: Farrar, Straus & Giroux, 1979.

Bloom, Paul. "No Smiting." Review of *The Evolution of God,* by Robert Wright, *New York Times,* June 28, 2009. https://www.nytimes.com/2009/06/28/books/review/Bloom-t. html.

Bonhoeffer, Dietrich. *Letters and Papers from Prison.* Edited by John W. de Gruchy. Translated by Isabel Best et al. Dietrich Bonhoeffer Works 8. Minneapolis: Fortress, 2010.

Borg, Marcus. *Meeting Jesus Again for the First Time.* San Francisco: HarperSanFrancisco, 1995.

Boyarin, Daniel, and Jonathan Boyarin. "Diaspora: Generation and Ground of Jewish Identity." *Critical Inquiry* 19 (1993) 693–725.

Braverman, Mark. *Fatal Embrace: Christians, Jews, and the Search for Peace in the Holy Land.* Austin: Synergy, 2010.

———. "A Prophetic Theology for the Present Kairos: Reflections on an Ecumenical Movement for the 21st Century." An unpublished paper delivered at the Volmoed Theological Colloquium on Christianity and Islam. August 2016.

———. "Remarks at Holy Land Ecumenical Foundation: The Role of Faith in Bringing Peace to the Middle East." Remarks delivered at the 11th Annual Meeting of the Holy Land Ecumenical Foundation on October 24, 2009. http://markbraverman.org/ writing/remarks-for-panel-on-the-role-of-faith-in-bringing-peace-to-the-middle-east.

———. *A Wall in Jerusalem: Hope, Healing, and the Struggle for Justice in Israel and Palestine.* New York: Jericho, 2013.

Bremer, Francis J. *Puritanism: A Very Short Introduction.* Very Short Introductions 212. New York: Oxford University Press, 2009.

Brown, Robert McAfee. "Christians in the West Must Confront the Middle East." In *Beyond Occupation: American Jewish, Christian, and Palestinian Voices for Peace,* edited by Rosemary Radford Ruether and Marc H. Ellis, 138–54. Boston: Beacon, 1990.

Brown, Stephen. "Theologians Warn on 'Biblical Metaphors' in Middle East Conflict." *Presbyterian Outlook,* September 16, 2008. https://pres-outlook.org/2008/09/ theologians-warn-on-biblical-metaphors-in-middle-east-conflict/.

Brueggemann, Walter. *Chosen? Reading the Bible amid the Israeli–Palestinian Conflict.* Louisville: Westminster John Knox, 2015.

———. "Reading the Bible amid the Israeli-Palestinian Conflict." *Theology Today* 73 (2016) 36–45.

Burg, Avraham. *The Holocaust Is Over: We Must Rise from Its Ashes.* New York: St. Martin's Griffin, 2016.

Burge, Gary M. *Whose Land? Whose Promise? What Christians Are not Being Told about Israel and the Palestinians.* Cleveland: Pilgrim, 2003.

Burke, Patrick. *Reinterpreting Rahner: A Critical Study of His Major Themes.* New York: Fordham University Press, 2002.

Byman, Daniel L. "Comparing Al Qaeda and ISIS: Different Goals, Different Targets." Prepared testimony before the Subcommittee on Counterterrorism and Intelligence of the House Committee on Homeland Security. Wednesday, April 29, 2015. https:// www.brookings.edu/testimonies/comparing-al-qaeda-and-isis-different-goals- different-targets.

Cahill, Thomas. *The Gifts of the Jews: How a Tribe of Desert Nomads Changed the Way Everyone Thinks.* New York: RosettaBooks, 2004.

Carroll, Sean. *The Big Picture: On the Origins of Life, Meaning, and the Universe Itself.* New York: Random House, 2016.

Chernus, Ira. *Monsters to Destroy: The Neoconservative War on Terror and Sin.* Boulder, CO: Paradigm, 2006.

———. "Three Myths of Israel's Insecurity." *Nation*, April 2011. https://www.thenation. com/article/archive/three-myths-israels-insecurity.

Close, Frank. *Particle Physics: A Very Short Introduction.* Very Short Introductions 109. Oxford: Oxford University Press, 2012.

Cobb, John, Jr., and David Ray Griffin. *Process Theology: An Introductory Exposition.* Louisville: Westminster John Knox, 1999.

Cohen, Robert A. H. "Dear Rabbi Sacks—Stop Your Lies about BDS." *Writing from the Edge: Rescuing the Hebrew Covenant One Blogpost at a Time* (blog), on Patheos (website), March 2, 2017. https://www.patheos.com/blogs/writingfromtheedge/2017/03/dear- rabbi-sacks-stop-lies-bds.

———. "Sacks v. Corbyn: Why Conflating Anti-Zionism Makes Fighting Antisemitism Impossible." *Writing from the Edge: Rescuing the Hebrew Covenant One Blogpost at a Time* (blog), on Patheos (website), September 2, 2018. https://www.patheos.com/ blogs/writingfromtheedge/2018/09/sacks-v-corbyn-why-conflating-anti-zionism- makes-fighting-antisemitism-impossible. Three Myths of Israel's Insecurity

———. "Thank You Chief Rabbi. Now I Know. Judaism Is to Blame for the Palestinian Nakba." *Writing from the Edge: Rescuing the Hebrew Covenant One Blogpost at a Time* (blog), on Patheos (website), May 15, 2016. https://www.patheos.com/blogs/ writingfromtheedge/2016/05/thank-you-chief-rabbi-now-i-know-judaism-is-to- blame-for-the-palestinian-nakba.

Collier, Paul, and Anke Hoeffler. "Greed and Grievance in Civil War." *Oxford Economic Papers* 56 (2004) 563–95, https://doi.org/10.1093/oep/gpf064.

Cone, James. *Black Theology and Black Power.* Rev. ed. Maryknoll, NY: Orbis, 1997.

Cooper, David E. *Existentialism: A Reconstruction.* 2nd ed. Introducing Philosophy 8. Oxford: Blackwell, 1999.

Crick, Francis. *The Astonishing Hypothesis: The Scientific Search for the Soul.* New York: Scribner, 1994.

Davidson, Richard, and Sharon Begley. *The Emotional Life of Your Brain: How Its Unique Patterns Affect the Way You Think, Feel, and Live—and How You Can Change Them.* London: Hodder & Stoughton, 2013.

Davies, Sally. "The Blind Spot: It's Tempting to Think Science Gives a God's Eye View of Reality." *Aeon* 8 January 2019. https://aeon.co/essays/the-blind-spot-of-science-is-the-neglect-of-lived-experience.

Davies, W. D. *The Gospel and the Land.* Berkeley: University of California Press, 1968.

Dawkins, Richard. *The God Delusion.* 1st Mariner Books ed. Boston: Houghton Mifflin, 2008.

———. "Meet My Cousin, the Chimpanzee." *New Scientist* (June 5, 1993). https://www.richarddawkins.net/2014/06/meet-my-cousin-the-chimpanzee.

———. *The Selfish Gene.* Oxford: Oxford University Press, 1989.

De Gruchy, John W. *Confessions of a Christian Humanist.* Minneapolis: Fortress, 2006.

———. *Led into Mystery: Faith Seeking Answers in Life and Death.* London: SCM, 2013.

———. "Reality and Mystery: Scientific Understanding, Christian Humanism, and Defining Moral Imperatives." *Journal of Theology for Southern Africa* 157 (March 2017) 59–70.

———. "Retrieving the Soul: Understanding the Soul as Dynamic and Relational." *Journal of Theology for Southern Africa* 149 (July 2014) 56–69.

Delong-Bas, Natana J. *Wahhabi Islam: From Revival and Reform to Global Jihad.* London: International Islamic Publishing House, 2010.

Derrida, Jacques. "'This Strange Institution Called Literature': An Interview with Jacques Derrida." In *Acts of Literature*, edited by Derek Attridge, 33–75. Translated by Nicholas Royle. London: Routledge, 1992. https://monoskop.org/images/9/9a/Derrida_Jacques_Acts_of_Literature_1992.pdf.

Dodds, E. R. *Pagan and Christian in the Age of Anxiety.* Cambridge: Cambridge University Press, 1968.

Druyan, Ann. "Ann Druyan, Talks about Science, Religion, Wonder, Awe . . . and Carl Sagan." *Skeptical Inquirer* 27.6 (2003) 25–30.

Dundes, Alan. *The Blood Libel Legend: A Casebook in Anti-Semitic Folklore.* Madison: University of Wisconsin Press, 1991.

Einstein, Albert. "Science and Religion." In *Science, Philosophy, and Religion: A Symposium*, n.p. New York: The Conference on Science, Philosophy, and Religion, 1941. See also https://www.update.uu.se/~fbendz/library/ae_scire.htm.

Ellis, Glenn, and Viktoryia Kolchyna. "Putin and the 'Triumph of Christianity' in Russia." *Reporter's Notebook* (blog), on *Al-Jazeera* (website), October 19, 2017. https://www.aljazeera.com/blogs/europe/2017/10/putin-triumph-christianity-russia-171018073916624.html.

Ellis, Marc H. *Beyond Innocence and Redemption.* New York: Harper & Row, 1990.

———. *Beyond Innocence & Redemption: Confronting the Holocaust and Israeli Power; Creating a Moral Future for the Jewish People.* 1990. Reprint, Eugene, OR: Wipf & Stock, 2016.

———. *Toward a Jewish Theology of Liberation.* London: SCM, 1987.

Esak, Farid. "Islam, Feminism and Empire: A Comparison between the Approaches of Amin Wadud and Saba Mahmood." *Journal of Gender and Religion in Africa* 24/1 (2015) 27–48.

———. *Qur'an, Liberation & Pluralism: An Islamic Perspective of Interreligious Solidarity against Oppression.* Oxford: Oneworld, 1997.

Esslin, Martin. *The Theatre of the Absurd*. London: Eyre & Spottiswoode, 1968.

Fackenheim, Emil. *To Mend the World: Foundation of Future Jewish Thought*. New York: Shocken, 1982.

Fanack.com (website). "Religions in the Middle East and North Africa." https://fanack. com/religions-in-the-middle-east-and-north-africa.

Fantz, Ashley. "Bin Laden's Letters Reveal a Terrorist Losing Control." *CNN* (website), May 4, 2012. http://edition.cnn.com/2012/05/03/us/bin-laden-documents/index. html.

Fenton, John W. "Early Lutherans and the Greek Church." *Orthodoxy and Heterodoxy* (blog), October 3, 2017. https://blogs.ancientfaith.com/orthodoxyandheterodoxy /2017/10/03/lutherans-greek-church.

Finkelstein, Israel, and Neil Ascher Silberman. *The Bible Unearthed: New Vision of Ancient Israel and the Origins of Its Sacred Texts*. New York: Simon & Schuster, 2002.

Fisk, Robert. *The Great War for Civilization: The Conquest of the Middle East*. New York: Vintage, 2007.

Folb, Peter. *Raindrops Are Falling*. Self-published. Cape Town: Imagovisual, 2018.

Gillespie, John. "Sartre and God: A Spiritual Odyssey? Part 1." *Sartre Studies International* 19, 2013.

———. "Sartre and God: A Spiritual Odyssey? Part 2." *Sartre Studies International* 20, 2014.

Gillis, David. "Introduction: A Portrait of the Artist 1–7 (Outline of the Cosmic Model of Mishneh Torah's Structure)." In *Reading Maimonides' "Mishneh Tora,"* 1–7. Oxford: Littman Library of Jewish Civilization, 2015. https://www.academia.edu/25632631/ Reading_Maimonides_Mishneh_Torah_Book_-_Introduction_A_Portrait_of_the_ Artist_1-7_Outline_of_the_Cosmic_Model_of_Mishneh_Torahs_Structure.

Gilson, Etienne. *History of Christian Philosophy in the Middle Ages*. New York: Random House, 1955.

Gray, John. *Seven Types of Atheism*. New York: Farrar, Straus & Giroux, 2018.

Greeley, Andrew. *Religion in Europe at the End of the Second Millennium*. New York: Routledge, 2017.

Green, Christopher. *Doxological Theology: Karl Barth on Divine Providence, Evil and the Angels*. London: Bloomsbury T. & T. Clark, 2013.

Greenberg, Irving. "Cloud of Smoke, Pillar of Fire: Judaism, Christianity and Modernity after the Holocaust." In *Auschwitz: Beginning of a New Era? Reflections on the Holocaust*, edited by Eva Fleischner, 7–55, 441–46. New York: Ktav, 1977. http:// rabbiirvinggreenberg.com/wp-content/uploads/2013/02/Cloud-of-Smoke-red.pdf.

Gutiérrez, Gustavo. *We Drink from Our Own Wells: The Spiritual Journey of a People*. Translated by Michael O'Connell. Maryknoll NY: Orbis, 1984.

Habermas, Jürgen. *An Awareness of What Is Missing: Faith and Reason in the Post-Secular Age*. Cambridge: Polity, 2010.

Harari, Yuval Noah. *Sapiens: A Brief History of Humankind*. New York: Harper Collins, 2015.

———. *21 Lessons for the 21st Century*. London: Cape, 2018.

———. "Work." In *21 Lessons for the 21st Century*, 20–43. London: Cape, 2018.

Hastings, Adrian, ed. *A World History of Christianity*. Grand Rapids: Eerdmans, 1999.

Haught, John. *God after Darwin: A Theology of Evolution*. 2nd ed. Boulder, CO: Westview, 2009.

Hawking, Stephen. *A Brief History of Time*. With a new foreword. New York: Bantam, 2017.

Helminski, Kabir. "Introduction." In *The Pocket Rumi*, edited by Kabir Helminski, ix–xiv. Boulder, CO: Shambhala, 2008.

Herman, Simon. *Israelis and Jews: A Study in the Continuity of an Identity*. New York: Random House, 1970.

Heschel, Abraham Joshua. *Israel: An Echo of Eternity*. New York: Farrar, Straus & Giroux, 1987.

———. *The Sabbath: Its Meaning for Modern Man*. 1951. Reprinted, with an introduction by Susannah Heschel. FSG Classics. New York: Farrar, Straus & Giroux, 2005.

Heschel, Susannah. Introduction to *The Sabbath: Its Meaning for Modern Man*, by Abraham Joshua Heschel, vii–xvi. FSG Classics. New York: Farrar, Straus & Giroux, 2005.

———. "Their Feet Were Praying." *New York Jewish Week*, January 10, 2012. https://jewishweek.timesofisrael.com/their-feet-were-praying/.

Holland, Tom. *Rubicon: Tragedy of the Roman Empire*. London: Abacus, 2010.

Homans, Jennifer. "Introduction." In *When the Facts Change: Essays (1995–2010)*, by Tony Judt, 1–10. Edited by Jennifer Homans. New York: Penguin, 2015.

Horsley, Richard, ed. *In the Shadow of Empire: Reclaiming the Bible as History*. Louisville: Westminster John Knox, 2008.

International Forum for Rights and Security. *ISIS: The Terror Empire*. Toronto: International Forum for Rights and Security, 2019.

Irvin, Dale T., and Scott W. Sunquist. *History of the World Christian Movement*. Vol.1, *Earliest Christianity to 1453*. Maryknoll, NY: Orbis, 2001.

James, Craig A. *The Religion Virus*. Self-published. 2nd ed. Lavergne, TN: CreateSpace, 2013.

Jáuregui, Pablo. "Stephen Hawking: 'No hay ningún dios. Soy ateo.'" Ciencia. Astrofísica. Enviado especial. Guía de Isora (Tenerife). *El Mundo*, March 14, 2018. https://www.elmundo.es/ciencia/2014/09/21/541dbc12ca474104078b4577.html.

Jenkins, Philip. *The Next Christendom*. New York: Oxford University Press, 2002.

Johnson, Elizabeth A. *She Who Is: The Mystery of God in Feminist Theological Discourse*. Twenty-fifth-anniversary ed. New York: Crossroad, 2017.

Jones, Seth G., et al. "The Escalating Terrorism Problem in the United States." CSIS Briefs. June 17, 2020. https://www.csis.org/analysis/escalating-terrorism-problem-united-states/.

Judt, Tony. *When the Facts Change: Essays (1995–2010)*. Edited and introduced by Jennifer Homans. New York: Penguin, 2015.

Juergensmeyer, Mark. *Global Rebellion: Religious Challenges to the Secular State, From Christian Militias to Al Qaeda*. Berkeley: University of California Press, 2008.

———. *Terror in the Mind of God: The Global Rise of Religious Violence*. Berkeley: University of California Press, 2003.

Jung, C. G., and R. F. C. Hull. *Four Archetypes. From the Collected Works of C. G. Jung*. Princeton: Princeton University Press, 1969. JStor. doi:10.2307/j.ctt7sw9v.

Kairos Theologians. *Challenge to the Church: The Kairos Document*. Johannesburg: Institute for Contextual Theology/Skotaville, 1985.

Kaufmann, Walter. *Existentialism from Dostoevsky to Sartre*. New York: Meridian, 1956.

Keen, Sam. *In the Absence of God: Dwelling in the Presence of the Sacred*. New York: Harmony, 2010.

Kelleher, Karen. "The Afternoon of Life: Jung's View of the Tasks of the Second Half of Life." *Perspectives in Psychiatric Care,* 28 April 2009. https://doi.org/10 .1111/j.1744-6163.1992.tb00367.x.

Keyscore, X. "Sunni Wahhabism vs. Shi'a Islam—Who Foments the Violence?" *X Keyscore's Blog* (blog) on Intellihub (website), March 2, 2016. https://www.intellihub. com/sunni-wahhabism-vs-shia-islam.

Khalidi, Rashid. *Brokers of Deceit: How the U.S. Has Undermined Peace in the Middle East.* Boston: Beacon, 2013.

Kierkegaard, Søren. *Attack upon "Christendom," 1854–1855.* Translated with an introduction by Walter Lowrie. Princeton: Princeton University Press, 1944.

———. *Concluding Unscientific Postscript to "Philosophical fragments."* Vol. 1. Edited and translated with introduction and notes by Howard V. Hong and Edna H. Hong. Kierkegaard's Writings 12. Princeton: Princeton University Press, 1992.

———. *Fear and Trembling.* Edited by C. Stephen Evans and Sylvia Walsh. Cambridge Texts in the History of Philosophy. Cambridge: Cambridge University Press, 2006.

Kipling, Rudyard. "The White Man's Burden." http://www.kiplingsociety.co.uk/poems_ burden.htm.

Kirkpatrick, Kate. *Sartre and Theology.* Philosophy and Theology 23. London: Bloomsbury T. & T. Clark, 2017.

Kirsch, Adam. Review of *Ancient Israel,* by Robert Alter. *Tablet,* June 12, 2013. http://www. tabletmag.com/jewish-arts-and-culture/books/134573/robert-alter-ancient-israel.

Kluger, Jeffrey. "This Is Your Brain on Creativity." In *The Science of Creativity,* by the editors of *Time,* 11–17. New York: Time, 2018.

Knight, Janice. *Orthodoxies in Massachusetts: Rereading American Puritanism.* Cambridge: Harvard University Press, 1997.

Kundera, Milan. *The Book of Laughter and Forgetting.* London: Faber & Faber, 1996.

Lamott, Anne. *Bird by Bird: Some Instructions on Writing and Life.* 1st Anchor Books ed. New York: Anchor, 1995.

Law, Stephen. "Wittgenstein and Religion." *Think,* 3 January 2019. https://aeon.co/essays/ atheists-vs-religious-belief-with-wittgenstein-on-the-stand.

Lawrence, Bruce B. *Defenders of God: The Fundamentalist Revolt against the Modern Age.* New York: Harper & Row, 1989.

Lenski, Noel. "Imperial Legislation and the Donatist Controversy: From Constantine to Honorius," in *The Donatist Schism: Controversy and Contexts,* edited by Richard Miles, 166–219. Liverpool: Liverpool University Press, 2016.

Lister, Charles. *Profiling the Islamic State.* Brookings Doha Center Analysis Paper 13. Washington, DC: Brookings Institution, 2014.

Livio, Mario. *Why? What Makes Us Curious.* New York: Simon & Schuster, 2007.

Lowney, Chris. *A Vanished World: Muslims, Christians and Jews in Medieval Spain.* New York: Oxford University Press, 2006.

Luther, Martin. *Works of Martin Luther with Introduction and Notes,* 2:179–85 6 vols. Translated by .J. J. Schindel and C. M. Jacobs. Philadelphia: Holman, 1915.

Maalouf, Amm. *The Crusades through Arab Eyes.* London: Folio Society, 2012.

Maimonides, Moses Ben. *Guide for the Perplexed.* Translated by M. Friedlander. 2nd ed., revised throughout. London: Routledge, 1904. http://www.teachittome.com/ seforim2/seforim/the_guide_for_the_perplexed.pdf.

———. *Misneh Torah: Yad Hazakah.* New York: Hebrew Publishing Company, 1989. https://www.wdl.org/en/item/3962/#q=Mishneh+Torah&qla=en.

Majid, Anouar. *We Are All Moors: Ending Centuries of Crusades against Muslims and Other Minorities.* Minneapolis: University of Minnesota Press, 2009.

Malik, Kenan. *The Quest for a Moral Compass: A Global History of Ethics.* London: Atlantic, 2015.

Marcus, Gary. "The Problem with the Neuroscience Backlash." Annals of Technology. *New Yorker,* June 19, 2013. https://www.newyorker.com/tech/elements/the-problem-with-the-neuroscience-backlash.

Marshall, Tim. *Divided: Why We're Living in an Age of Walls.* London: Elliott &Thompson, 2018.

Mastrantonis, George. *Augsburg and Constantinople: The Correspondence between the Tübingen Theologians and Patriarch Jeremiah II of Constantinople on the Augsburg Confession.* The Archbishop Iakovos Library of Ecclesiastical and Historical Sources 7. Brookline, MA: Holy Cross Orthodox Press, 1982.

McCullum, Ian. "The Pulse of Protest." *Africa Geographic* 14/3, April 2006.

McFague, Sallie. *The Body of God: An Ecological Theology.* Minneapolis: Fortress, 1993.

McGilchrist, Iain. *The Master and His Emissary: The Divided Brain and the Making of the Modern World.* New Haven: Yale University Press, 2012.

Mda, Zakes. *Justify the Enemy: Becoming Human in South Africa.* Edited and introduced by J. U. Jacobs. Pietermaritzburg: University of Kwa-Zulu Natal Press, 2018.

Mearns, W. Hughes. "The Little Man Who Wasn't There." 1899. https://www.poets.org/poetsorg/poem/antigonish-i-met-man-who-wasnt-there.

Mencken, H. L. "Memorial Service." Quoted in "A Memorial Service for Dead Gods . . . or Their Followers?" (blog post). In *Brahma Kumaris Info—The Truth about BK Meditation: Independent Thought about the Brahma Kumaris World Spiritual University* (website), 16 November 2014. http://brahmakumaris.info/forum/viewtopic.php?f=12&t=3576/.

Merton, Thomas. *The Seven Storey Mountain.* New York: Harcourt, 1948.

Metz, Johann Baptist. *Faith in History and Society: Towards a Practical Fundamental Theology.* New York: Seabury, 1980.

Michalson, Carl. *The Hinge of History: An Existential Approach to the Christian Faith.* New York: Scribner, 1959.

Milligan, Jeffrey Ayala. *Teaching in the Presence of Burning Children: Attending to Tragedy and Faith in Philosophy and Education.* http://files.eric.ed.gov/fulltext/EJ775216.pdf.

Mirvis, Ephraim. "Ken Livingstone and the Hard Left Are Spreading the Insidious Virus of Anti-Semitism." *Telegraph,* May 3, 2016. https://www.telegraph.co.uk/news/2016/05/03/ken-livingstone-and-the-hard-left-are-spreading-the-insidious-vi.

Moghaddam, Fathali. *Mutual Radicalization: How Groups and Nations Drive Each Other to Extremes.* Washington, DC: American Psychological Association, 2018.

Moosa, Ebrahim. *Ghazali and the Poetics of Imagination.* Chapel Hill: University of North Carolina Press, 2005.

———. "Political Theology in the Aftermath of the Arab Spring: Returning to the Ethical." In *The African Renaissance and the Afro-Arab Spring: A Season of Rebirth?,* edited by Charles Villa-Vicencio et al., 101–19. Washington, DC: Georgetown University Press, 2014.

———. *What Is a Madrasa?* Chapel Hill: University of North Carolina Press, 2015.

Moussalli, Ahmad. "Wahhabism, Salafism and Islamism: Who is the Enemy?" http://conflictsforum.org/briefings/Wahhabism-Salafism-and-Islamism.pdf.

Moore, Edward. "Origen of Alexandria." *Internet Encyclopedia of Philosophy.* https://iep. utm.edu/origen-of-alexandria/.

Moyers, Bill. Interview with Robert Wright. https://www.youtube.com/watch?v=Jis N9t504IU.

———. *The Wisdom of Faith with Huston Smith* (a five-part series). Directed and produced by Pamela Mason Wagner. DVD. The Bill Collection. Princeton: Films for the Humanities & Sciences, 1996.

Murata, Sachiko, and William C. Chittick. *Vision of Islam: Reflecting on the Hadith of Gabriel.* New York: Paragon, 1994.

Na'im, Abdullahi. *Islam and Human Rights: Selected Essays of Abdullahi An-Na'im.* Edited by Mashood A Baderin. Collected Essays in Law. Brookfield, VT: Taylor & Francis, 2010.

———. *What Is an American Muslim? Embracing Faith and Citizenship.* Oxford: Oxford University Press, 2014.

Nasr, Vali. *The Shia Revival.* New York: Norton, 2007.

National Geographic Society. "Map of Human Migration." *Genographic Project* (blog), on *National Geographic* (website).

Niebuhr, Reinhold. *Moral Man and Immoral Society.* New York: Scribner, 1932.

———. "The Relevance of an Impossible Ethical Idea." In *Interpretation of Christian Ethics,* 101–36. New York: Harper, 1935.

———. *Why the Christian Church Is not Pacifist.* London: SCM, 1940.

Nietzsche, Friedrich. *The Gay Science.* Translated with commentary by Walter Kaufmann. Vintage Books edition. New York: Random House, 1974. https://philoslugs.files. wordpress.com /2016/12/the-gay-science-friedrich-nietzsche.pdf.

Nolan, Albert. *Jesus before Christianity.* Maryknoll, NY: Orbis, 1978.

Noor Foundation International Inc. *The Holy Qur'an: Arabic Text–English Translation.* 3rd ed. Hockessin, DE: Noor Foundation International Inc., 2013.

Oates, Joyce Carol. *The Faith of a Writer: Life, Craft, Art.* New York: HarperCollins, 2003.

Olson, Steve. *Mapping Human History: Genes, Race and Our Common Origins.* New York: Mariner, 2003.

O'Murchu, Diarmuid. *God in the Midst of Change: Wisdom for Confusing Times.* Maryknoll, NY: Orbis, 2013.

———. *Quantum Theology: Spiritual Implications of the New Physics.* New York: Crossroad, 1998.

Osborne, Hannah. "E. O. Wilson: I'm not an Atheist but Religion Should Be Eliminated." Science/Environment, *International Business Times,* January 28, 2015. https://www. ibtimes.co.uk/e-o-wilson-im-not-atheist-religion-should-be-eliminated-1485543.

Oppy, Graham. "Ontological Arguments." In *Stanford Encyclopedia of Philosophy* (website). First published Thu Feb 8, 1996; substantive revision Wed Feb 6, 2019. https://plato.stanford.edu/entries/ontological-arguments.

Otto, Rudolf. *The Idea of the Holy.* Translated by John W. Harvey. 2nd ed. 1958. Reprint, Mansfield, CT: Martino, 2010.

Pew Research Center for Religion and Public Life. *Religious Landscape Study.* https:// www.pewforum.org/religious-landscape-study.

———. "Why Do Levels of Religious Observance Vary by Age and Country?" In *The Age Gap in Religion around the World.* Pew Forum. https://www.pewforum.org/2018/ 06/13/why-do-levels-of-religious-observance-vary-by-age-and-country.

Pinker, Steven. *Enlightenment Now: The Case for Reason, Science, Humanism and Progress.* London: Lane, 2018.

Porter, J. M., ed. *Luther: His Political Writings.* Philadelphia: Fortress, 1974.

Quammen, David. *The Tangled Tree: A Radical New History of Life.* New York: Simon & Schuster, 2019.

Quote Investigator (website). "Two Things Are Infinite: the Universe and Human Stupidity." May 4, 2010. https://quoteinvestigator.com/2010/05/04/universe-einstein.

Raheb, Mitri. *Faith in the Face of Empire: The Bible through Palestinian Eyes.* Maryknoll, NY: Orbis, 2014.

Rahner, Karl. *Hearers of the Word.* New York: Herder & Herder, 1969.

Rasool, Ebrahim. "Charlie Hebdo: Who Has Dishonoured the Prophet?" *World For All,* 10 January 2015.

———. Unpublished manuscript, Chapter 4. 2014.

Reynolds, Terrence. "Was Erasmus Responsible for Luther? A Study of the Relationship of the Two Reformers and Their Clash over the Question of the Will." *Concordia Theological Journal* 41/4 (1977) 18–34.

Richardson, Peter, and Robert Boyd. *Not By Genes Alone: How Culture Transformed Human Evolution.* Chicago: University of Chicago Press, 2005.

Rohr, Richard, OFM. "Belief or Discipleship?" (daily meditation). January 22, 2019. Following Jesus (meditation series). https://cac.org/belief-or-discipleship-2019-01-22.

———. "An Evidence-Based Emergence" (daily meditation). November 5, 2019. https://cac.org/an-evidence-based-emergence-2019-11-05.

———. "The Franciscan Way: Beyond the Bird Bath" (course description). https://cac.org/online-ed/franciscan-way-course-description.

———. "Many Ways of Knowing" (daily meditation). January 8, 2019. https://cac.org/many-ways-of-knowing-2019-01-08.

———. "Practical Christianity" (daily meditation). January 24, 2019. Following Jesus (mediation series). https://cac.org/practical-christianity-2019-01-24.

Rubenstein, Richard. *After Auschwitz.* Indianapolis: Bobbs-Merrill, 1968.

———. *The Cunning of History.* New York: Harper & Row, 1975.

Rushd, Ibn. *Beyond Fundamentalism: Confronting Religious Extremism in the Age of Globalization.* New York: Random House, 2009.

———. *On the Meaning of Religion and Philosophy.* Translated by George Hourani, 1961. https://www.aub.edu.lb/fas/cvsp/Documents/reading_selections/CVSP%20202/Fall%202012-2013/CVSP%20202%20Ibn%20Rushd.pdf.

Sacks, Jonathan. "Darwin." In *The Great Partnership: Science, Religion and the Search for Meaning,* 209–32. New York: Schocken, 2011.

———. *The Great Partnership: Science, Religion, and the Search for Meaning.* New York: Schocken, 2011.

———. "When Religion Goes Wrong." In *The Great Partnership: Science, Religion, and the Search for Meaning,* 249–266. New York: Schocken, 2011.\

———. "Why God?" In *The Great Partnership: Science, Religion, and the Search for Meaning,* 267–91. New York: Schocken, 2011.

Sagan, Carl. *Cosmos.* New York: Random House, 2002.

———. *The Demon-Haunted World: Science as Candle in the Dark.* New York: Random House, 1996.

———. *The Dragons of Eden: Speculations on the Evolution of Human Intelligence.* New York: Random House, 1977.

————. *Pale Blue Dot: A Vision of the Human Future in Space.* New York: Ballantine, 1994.

————. *The Varieties of Scientific Experience: A Personal View of the Search for God.* Edited by Ann Druyan. With illustrations editor and scientific consultant Steven Soter. New York: Penguin, 2007.

Sagan, Carl, and Ann Druyan. *Comet.* New York: Ballantine, 1997.

Sagan, Carl, et al. *The Varieties of Scientific Experience.* New York: Penguin, 2007.

Said, Edward. *Orientalism.* London: Penguin, 2003.

Salvatore, Armando. *The Sociology of Islam: Knowledge, Power, Civility.* Hoboken, NJ: Wiley, 2016.

Satel, Sally, and Scott O. Lilienfeld. *Brainwashed: The Seductive Appeal of Mindless Neuroscience.* New York: Basic Books, 2015.

Sartre, Paul. *No Exit, and Three Other Plays.* New York: Vintage, 1989. https://www.vanderbilt.edu/olli/class-materials/Jean-Paul_Sartre.pdf.

Schüller, Werner. "Tillich's Life and Works." In *The Cambridge Companion to Paul Tillich*, edited by Russell Re Manning, 3–17. Cambridge Companions to Religion. Cambridge University Press, 2008.

Scruton, Roger. "Neurononsense and the Soul." In *Search of Self: Interdisciplinary Perspectives on Personhood*, edited by Wentzel van Huyssteen and Erik P. Wiebe, 338–56. Grand Rapids: Eerdmans, 2011.

Shaikh, Sa'diyya. *Sufi Narratives of Intimacy: Ibn 'Arab, Gender and Sexuality.* Chapel Hill: University of North Carolina Press, 2012.

Shain, Milton. *Antisemitism.* London: Bowerdean, 1998.

Shavit, Ari. *My Promised Land: The Triumph and Tragedy of Israel.* London: Scribe, 2018.

Shermer, Michael. "The Skeptic's Chaplain." *Skeptic Magazine* 1/2 (2007).

————"A Voyager in the Cosmos: An Interview with Ann Druyan." *Skeptic Magazine* 13/1 (2007) 20–26.

————. "Why Is There Something Rather Than Nothing?" *Skeptic Magazine* 23/4 (2018) 8–16.

Solomon, Robert C. *Existentialism.* New York: McGraw-Hill, 1974.

Soloveitchik, Joseph B. "Sacred and Profane: *Kodesh* and *Chol* in World Perspective." *Gesher* 3/1 (1966) 5–29.

————. "Sacred and Profane: *Kodesh* and *Chol* in World Perspective." *Jewish Thought* 3/1 (1993) 55–82.

Smith, Huston. *The World's Religions: Our Great Wisdom Traditions.* 50th anniversary ed. New York: HarperOne, 2009.

Smith, Morton. "Zealots and Sicarii, Their Origins and Relation." *Harvard Theological Review* 64 (1971) 1–19.

Smock, David. "Special Report: *Ijtihad*; Reinterpreting Islamic Principles for the Twenty-First Century." Summary of a panel cosponsored by the United States Institute of Peace and the Center for the Study of Democracy and held on March 19, 2004. https://www.usip.org/sites/default/files/sr125.pdf.

Starr, Mirabai. *God of Love: A Guide to the Heart of Judaism, Christianity and Islam.* Rhinebeck, NY: Monkfish, 2013.

Tayob, Abdulkader. *A Journey through Critical and Philosophical Reconstructions of Islam* (Unpublished). Based on 2019 Summer School lectures at the University of Cape Town.

Tearle, Oliver. "A Short Analysis of Emily Dickinson's 'Tell all the Truth but tell it slant.'" *Interesting Literature* (website). November 2016. https://interestingliterature.com/2016/11/a-short-analysis-of-emily-dickinsons-tell-all-the-truth-∂but-tell-it-slant.

Teilhard de Chardin, Pierre. *The Phenomenon of Man*. New York: Harper, 1961.

Thomas Aquinas. *Summa Theologica*, II,II, Article 7. In *Aquinas: Selected Political Writings*, edited by A. P. d'Entreves. Oxford: Blackwell, 1948.

Thomas, Elizabeth Marshall. *The Old Way: A Story of the First People*. New York: Picador, 2006.

Tillich, Paul. *The Courage to Be*. New Haven: Yale University Press, 1952.

Tocqueville, Alexis de. *Democracy in America*. Chicago: University of Chicago Press, 2000.

Trimble, Michael. *The Soul of the Brain*. Baltimore: Johns Hopkins University Press, 2007.

Tuchman, Barbara. *The March of Folly: From Troy to Vietnam*. London: Abacus, 1985.

Tylor, Edward Burnett. *Primitive Culture*. London: Murray, 1871. http://www.tbm100. org/Lib/Tyl20PC2.pdf/

Van Huyssteen, J. Wentzel. *Alone in the World? Human Uniqueness in Science and Theology*. Grand Rapids: Eerdmans, 2006.

Varela, Francisco J., et al. *Embodied Mind: Cognitive Science and Human Experience*. Boston: MIT Press, 1992.

Wallace, Catherine M. *Confronting Religious Denial of Science*. Eugene, OR: Cascade, 2016.

Ward, Keith. *More Than Matter? Is There More to Life Than Molecules?* Grand Rapids: Eerdmans, 2010.

Watson, Lyle. *Beyond Supernature: A New Natural History of the Supernatural*. New York: Bantam, 1987.

Whitelam, Keith. *The Invention of Ancient Israel: The Silencing of Palestinian History*. London, Routledge, 1996.

Whitman, Walt. "Preface to the 1855 second edition of *Leaves of Grass*." In *An 1855–56 Notebook toward the second edition of "Leaves of grass."* With an introduction and notes by Harold W. Blodgett; with a foreword by Charles E. Feinberg; additional notes by William White. Carbondale: Southern Illinois University Press, 1959.

Wiesel, Elie. *Night*. Translated by Stella Rodway. 1964. Reprint, New York: Avon, 1964.

Wilkens, Robert Louis. *First Thousand Years: A Global History of Christianity*. New Haven: Yale University Press, 2012.

Wilson, Edward O. *Consilience: The Unity of Knowledge*. New York: Vintage, 1998. http://www.wtf.tw/ref/wilson.pdf.

———. *Genesis: The Deep Origin of Societies*. New York: Liveright, 2019.

———. *The Origins of Creativity*. New York: Norton, 2017.

Withnall, Adam. "Pope Francis Declares Evolution and the Big Bang Theory Are Real, and God Is not 'a Magician with a Magic Wand.'" *Independent*, 28 October 2014. https://www.independent.co.uk/news/world/europe/pope-francis-declares-evolution-and-big-bang-theory-are-right-and-god-isn-t-magician-magic-wand-9822514.html.

Wright, Lawrence. *The Terror Years: From Al-Qaeda to the Islamic State*. New York: Knopf, 2016.

Wright, Robert. *Nonzero: The Logic of Human Destiny*. New York: Vintage, 2001.

———. *The Evolution of God: The Origins of Our Beliefs*. London: Little, Brown, 2009.

Yeats, William Butler. "The Second Coming." *Poetry Foundation*. https://www.poetryfoundation.org/poems/43290/the-second-coming.

Yonck, Richard. *Heart of the Machine: Our Future in a World of Artificial Emotional Intelligence*. New York: Arcade, 2017.

Zehr, Nahed Artoul. *The War against al-Qaeda: Religion, Policy, and Counter-narrative*. Washington, DC: Georgetown University Press, 2017.